Precious, Precocious Moments

Precious, Precocious Moments

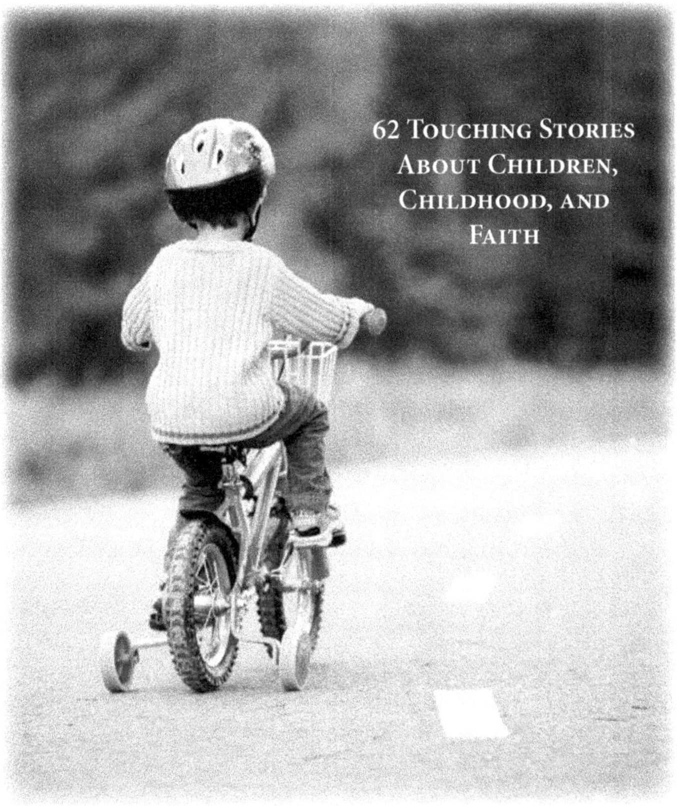
62 Touching Stories
About Children,
Childhood, and
Faith

Compiled and Edited by Yvonne Lehman

Grace Publishing
Broken Arrow, OK

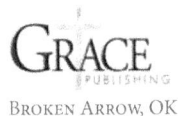

Scripture quotations marked NIV are taken from the *The Holy Bible, New International Version.* Copyright © 1973, 1978, 1984, International Bible Society. Used by permission of Zondervan. All rights reserved.

Scripture quotations marked NLT are taken from the *Holy Bible, New Living Translation,* copyright © 1996. Used by permission of Tyndale House Publishers, Inc., Wheaton, Illinois 60189. All rights reserved.

Scripture quotations marked NKJV taken from the *New King James Version®.* Copyright © 1982 by Thomas Nelson. Used by permission. All rights reserved.

Scripture quotations marked NASB are taken from the *New American Standard Bible®,* © Copyright 1960, 1962, 1963, 1968, 1971, 1972, 1973, 1975, 1977 The Lockman Foundation. Used by permission.

Scripture quotations marked ESV are taken from *The Holy Bible, English Standard Version* Copyright © 2001 by Crossway Bibles, a division of Good News Publishers. Used by permission.

Scripture quotations marked AMP are taken from the *Amplified Bible.* Copyright © 1954, 1958, 1962, 1964, 1965, 1987 by The Lockman Foundation. Used by permission.

PRECIOUS, PRECOCIOUS MOMENTS
62 TOUCHING STORIES ABOUT CHILDREN, CHILDHOOD, AND FAITH

ISBN-13: 978-1-60495-015-1

Copyright © 2015 by Yvonne Lehman. Published in the USA by Grace Publishing. All rights reserved. No part of this book may be reproduced in any form or by any electronic or mechanical means, including information storage and retrieval systems, without permission in writing, except as provided by USA Copyright law.

From Samaritan's Purse

We so appreciate you donating royalties from the sale of the books *Divine Moments, Christmas Moments, Spoken Moments* and *Precious, Precocious Moments* to Samaritan's Purse. What a blessing that you would think of us! Thank you for your willingness to bless others and bring glory to God through your literary talents. Grace and peace to you.

Their mission statement:

Samaritan's Purse is a nondenominational evangelical Christian organization providing spiritual and physical aid to hurting people around the world.

Since 1970, Samaritan's Purse has helped victims of war, poverty, natural disasters, disease, and famine with the purpose of sharing God's love through his son, Jesus Christ.

Go and do likewise. (Luke 10:37d)

You can learn more by visiting their website at www.samaritanspurse.org.

Dedication

Dedicated to
Terri Kalfas, who saw the beauty
and value of sharing praise in
Divine Moments
Christmas Moments
Spoken Moments
and now makes it possible
for the sharing of special
Precious, Precocious Moments

and

to all my children
Lori, Lisa, David, Cindy
(extended family: Rodney, Kellie, Steve, Yvonne M., Alma)
Sponsored: Another Cindy, Christian, Yuliati, Marie
Grands: John, Paul, Emily, Stephen, Rebekah,
Luke, Savannah, Simon, Celeste
On the way: all the lovely ones to follow
And all the precious, precocious little ones everywhere

and

to the writers who were so eager to share
without compensation
just thrilled to be useful
and be part of the mission work of
Samaritan's Purse

Contents

Introduction 9
1. Expect the Unexpected *Yvonne Lehman* 11
2. It Was Worth It *Greg M. Dodd* 16
3. Simply Brilliant *Jean Wilund* 18
4. Listen and Hear *Ann Knowles* 20
5. The Legend of the Weeping Willow *Felicity Younts* 22
6. A Battle with the Mouse King *Vicki H. Moss* 23
7. The Runaway *Kevin Spencer* 27
8. Wha'cha Doin, Mom? *Debbie Presnell* 29
9. A Land Where Magic Grows *Susan Engebrecht* 30
10. Mommy, You Stop It! *Autumn Conley* 32
11. Art of Communicating *Yvonne Lehman* 35
12. All God's Children *Sandra Fischer* 39
13. Uninvited Visitor (Eurajoki) *Mirjam Budarz* 41
14. The Accident *David Lehman* 46
15. Walking, Fixing, and Transforming *Susan Dollyhigh* 47
16. Food, Fun, and Fireworks *Helen L. Hoover* 50
17. Only in Our Hearts *Rob Buck* 52
18. From One Stage to Another *Yvonne Lehman* 56
19. The Guatemala Mission *Joann M. Claypoole* 59
20. God Rocks *Autumn Conley* 64
21. Name Them One by One *Cindy Wilson* 67
22. Tripping Over Alligators *C. Kevin Thompson* 69
23. Rich in Love *Virginia Foreman* 73
24. The Think Blessing *Yvonne Lehman* 75
25. Don't Be an Artist *Christina Krost* 77
26. Barren but Filled *Jessica Satterfield* 79
27. Backwards Party in a Hoghouse *Janice D. Green* 81
28. Bowling, Fishing, and Dancing *Susan Dollyhigh* 83
29. The Hollows of Our Hearts *Shirley G. Brosius* 86
30. The House That God Built *Ann Tatlock* 88
31. God Hasn't Given Me a Daddy Yet *Autumn Conley* 90

32. Foot-in-Mouth Problem *Yvonne Lehman* 92
33. This I Know *Tracy Crump* 96
34. A Mother's Heart *Diana Leagh Matthews* 99
35. I Am *Emily Marett* 102
36. The Potholder *Vicki H. Moss* 103
37. Joni *Judith Victoria Hensley* 105
38. Can't Live Here Anymore *Carolyn Barnum* 108
39. Comparisons *Carol Weeks* 111
40. My Best Name *Karen R. Hessen* 113
41. The Game *Veronica Leigh* 116
42. The Common Pot *Yvonne Lehman* 118
43. When Faith Flickers *Joey Rudder* 121
44. Steps *Robin Bayne* 124
45. Hinin' from de Sunder *Connie Gatlin* 125
46. The Roses *Elsie H. Brunk* 127
47. The Little Red Wheelbarrow *Beverly Hill McKinney* 129
48. First Things *Steve Wilson* 131
49. The Mind of a Child *Julie A. Hilton* 133
50. The Lesson *Diana Owens* 136
51. Motherhood: Living the Dream *Karen Sawyer* 138
52. Don't Forget to Pray *Autumn Conley* 140
53. The Old Bayonet *Thomas Kienzle* 142
54. What's a Grit? *Yvonne Lehman* 145
55. Katelyn's Cross *Susan Dollyhigh* 148
56. My Huckleberry Friend *Lydia E. Harris* 150
57. Cow Creamer *Mirjam Budarz* 153
58. Grandchild Journal, Legacy of Love *Elsie H. Brunk* 156
59. Cat Funerals *Vicki Moss* 160
60. I Dreamed a Dream *Carole Anne Pearson* 162
61. All Shook Up *Yvonne Lehman* 164
62. You Are Beautiful *Cindy Wilson* 167
About the Authors 169

Introduction

> The soul is healed by being with children.
> Fyodor Dostoyevsky

Precious, Precocious Moments turned out to be quite different than I had envisioned. It is the fourth in the Moments series, following *Divine Moments, Christmas Moments,* and *Spoken Moments.*

I thought this one would be lighter, perhaps a compilation of cute, delightful, humorous sayings and actions of those precious little ones that would entertain the reading audience. Many are just that. Others are not.

As authors began to respond to the call-out for articles or one-liners with a focus on children, I began to see the value of their contributions.

Yes, there are the delightful, entertaining stories that exemplify the beauty, innocence, and faith of a child. Then there are the stories that tug at the heart, which reminded me that a child suffers and grieves, has difficulty with his or her faith, just as adults do when questioning what God is doing or whether he is there or even cares.

These stories run the gamut of emotions, including laughter, love, loss, acceptance, forgiveness, grief, longing, despair, thankfulness, joy, courage, adults teaching children, children teaching adults, and best of all the awareness that God does indeed know and care, and if we seek him, we find him, because he was waiting for us all along with open arms, ready to show us the beauty in life — and that often comes through a little child.

Children make a difference in our lives as we do in theirs.

Just as in the other Moments books, the authors of these articles have generously donated their time and stories. They knew they would not receive monetary compensation but they have experienced what we all do, a sense of peace and joy when we give without expecting anything in return. Yet, we do expect something because we know God blesses, and in unexpected, wonderful ways. We're already blessed and thrilled that all royalties from the sale of this book will go to a worthy organization, Samaritan's Purse, whose ministry includes shoeboxes delivered throughout the world to children. And those boxes make a lasting spiritual impact on those children.

Regardless of our age, we all are God's children. Let us rejoice in that!

Yvonne Lehman

1
Expect the Unexpected

> Today it rained gorillas
> The rain looked like dinosaurs,
> It made dragons grow.
> I like the rain
> Because I like it.
> ~ *David Lehman* (age 7)

Hold onto the umbrella! My son's poem was like a foreshadowing of our family of four children and two parents. In our household it never rained cats and dogs. It rained gorillas!

For me, the process of having and nurturing children, watching their growth process, and sharing in their successes and failures was a maturing process, to say the least.

I was all set to be the perfect mother — rearing her perfect children — in an imperfect world. I had everything I needed to be a successful mother: books on parenting, magazines expounding the joys of motherhood, a loving responsible husband, and a reasonable intelligence of my own.

To me, young mothers who claimed they never slept, were distraught over the terrible twos, had no time to themselves and said, "Wait until you have children and you'll understand what it's all about," only meant that those women didn't know how to handle parenting.

My confidence soared. After becoming pregnant, and gaining only four pounds in the first three months, I nevertheless donned my maternity clothes, leaned back to walk like a banty hen, strutted like a rooster in charge of the barnyard and crowed to anyone who listened that any woman who didn't have that big bulge in front of her was out of shape.

My husband Howard, over a decade older than I, had warned, "You don't go into marriage or parenting, expecting sunny skies all year long." But I, a romantic, reveled in the adage, "Love conquers all."

There were times when storm clouds threatened, but the most amazing thing was how one whole dreamland of fantasy could be threatened with one simple statement.

After three years of marriage our first child was born. Howard walked through the hospital doorway, smiled proudly, came over and stared at the baby a long moment, then eyed me suspiciously and asked, "How did you and I, being Caucasian, come up with an Indian?"

Even I, who refused to believe that all newborn babies are red, wrinkly, and look alike, could not mistake the remarkable resemblance of our little one to that of a caricature of a papoose.

Her face had a triangular effect — perhaps one would call it pear-shaped. She sported a wide jawline, fat puffy cheeks, high cheekbones and a narrow forehead. Her red face was framed by black, straight hair that hung on each side in irregular strands below her ears but stood up on top about three inches, stiff as a brush, refusing to be combed down.

Feeling as if a storm cloud had appeared on my blue horizon, I could only manage to reply, "That's not what the ideal husband says in the movies."

Nevertheless, Lori was beautiful. She had a cute way of pursing her lips into a tight, firm pucker each time she had enough of her milk. Nothing could pry those lips apart, not even tickling the bottoms of her feet.

After two weeks, she unpursed her lips. She opened her mouth and hasn't closed it since.

I had a strange feeling nothing was ever going to be the same.

It wasn't!

I remember distinctly the day I threatened my own child...and followed through. I stopped putting the vitamins in her orange juice and began putting them in my coffee.

I had waded through two gallons of milk in one day, (milk baths aren't all that luxurious!) and swept up half a dozen broken glass bottles she had thrown to the floor. All the time I was telling myself, "I'm an adult. I'm the mother. She's just a helpless baby that can't talk, can't walk." Ah...I hit upon the solution.

With new vigor at having learned something the hard way, but knowing how to correct it, I told her, "You didn't win this one."

Later, I presented her with a brand new plastic bottle. She didn't even attempt to throw it, but meekly lay down on her back with the full bottle of milk, smiled broadly, exposed two shiny new upper teeth to match the two bottom ones and promptly bit off the end of the nipple.

As we progressed from the bottle to food, I prepared for that great challenge — trying to get food into her mouth. I bought bibs, hoping to protect her clothes. Ready, I sat down with a baby-food jar.

To my surprise, she opened her mouth like a baby bird anticipating its worm. What were those books talking about, I wondered? This was easy.

Then, with mouth full, she raised her head. And sneezed. Upward.

I looked up and winced as my daughter smiled. Did the baby books say anything about cleaning strained beets from the ceiling?

But…we did not have the choking problems of baby swallowing too much food at one time, or neglecting to chew bites of solid food. Oh, no! Nothing so ordinary. Mine went the longer route. Lori stuffed her cut-up bits of food up her nose and we had to make an emergency run to the hospital to remove her liver (from her nose).

Our second child, Lisa, born two years later, was much more discreet and possessed a high-class taste. She crawled around and found overlooked pieces of a broken necklace that even the vacuum cleaner had missed. No liver up the nose for her. She chose shiny, round pearls!

We had no such problems with our third child, born two years later. Our first boy — David. The girls wouldn't let him have anything or do anything. Sibling rivalry, I could readily see, would never allow him to grow up without feeling inferior because the two girls were never "on his side."

He possessed a more gentle nature than the girls and we felt it only fair to give him a brother to sort of even things out.

I should have suspected something when the fourth child refused to be born at nine months, but hung on for three more weeks, weighing almost ten pounds at birth.

We named him Cindy!

So, parenting wasn't turning out to be as perfect as I'd envisioned.

Each child was different, with varying needs, personality traits, abilities, and characteristics.

The books and magazines generalized, and that was helpful. But they couldn't cover the uniqueness of my children. Who had time to read anyway, or could afford the subscriptions? So I tossed them. (The magazines, not the children!)

I thought of the difficulty of rearing four different children when I was only beginning to mature as an adult. I was a child too — a child in the faith.

When each of my children said their first word, "No," I thought how it hurt my heart and pondered how many times had I hurt the heart of God by saying, "No."

How many times had I done the equivalent of throwing a bottle daily — sometimes by commission and sometimes by omission — and pursing my lips instead of obeying what God told me to do? How many times had I made a mess of things, even worse than inadvertently sneezing beets on the ceiling?

God loved me anyway. And I loved my children anyway. Just as God did with me, I continued to love and nurture them.

God knew it wouldn't always be smooth sailing. That's why he gave us his book of instruction.

Trying to follow the teachings of a very wise teacher, I took as my guide the verse of Proverbs 22:6: *Train up a child in the way he should go, and when he is older, he will not depart from it.* (NKJV) Fortunately, I didn't really stop to think how many years lay between "train up" and "older."

The children definitely presented unexpected challenges daily. The "training up" task seemed insurmountable. Particularly in answering some of their questions.

One day, the 2 ½-year-old was singing, "Jesus loves me this I know, for the Bible tells me so. Little ones to him belong."

Suddenly she stopped singing, looked up at me in all innocence and asked, "Mommy, why does he want us to be 'long'?"

I think back upon those days and smile. I see also the years that passed all too quickly. Questions and answers (which I didn't always have) became more serious. Day-to-day living brings us face to face with tough times, decisions and relationships that require patience, love, stamina, and holding onto our umbrella of faith in God.

Yes, there were gorillas, dinosaurs, dragons, and rain.
But I'd do it all again.
Because I liked it.

- Yvonne Lehman

Anyone who listens to my teaching and obeys me is wise,
like a person who builds a house on a solid rock.
Though the rain comes in torrents
And the floodwaters rise and the winds beat against that house,
it won't collapse, because it is built on a rock.
Jesus (Matthew 7:24-25)

2
It Was Worth It

By the year my son, Hampton, turned fourteen, he and I had become avid skimboard enthusiasts. Most of our days on the beach that summer were spent standing before the ocean, skimboard in hand, waiting for the next wave to wash a thin layer of warm water across the sand, followed by an all-out sprint, a quick step onto our boards, and a smooth glide across the faintest edge of the green Atlantic. All day. The thirty-second shot of adrenalin from each ride became an addiction that pushed us past fatigue and good sense. But it was a joyful, shared addiction.

Late on the afternoon that July 4th, after hours of skimming up and down the beach, I posed a new idea. Rather than skimming parallel to the waves, we would ride into them as they washed away from us. Less running back and forth, I reasoned. Also, a new thrill awaited. With a quick turn into an approaching wave, we could briefly transition from skimming to surfing. "That's how they do it in California," I explained. Hampton agreed. So, tired but excited, we turned our attention to the oncoming waves.

Seeing the first opportunity a moment later, I tossed my board before me only to see it speed away with the retreating water. I raced to catch up. My feet found the board just before hitting the face of the curling wave. I had no time to turn. The speed, the board, and the wave combined to launch me high into the air. As I watched my feet rotate slowly over my head, a young boy swimming nearby shouted, "Whoa!" I knew I was in trouble.

Upside down and descending, I closed my eyes, stretched my arms over my head, and braced for impact. At least I was over water, I thought. But the passing wave had taken most of the depth with it, leaving only about a foot to soften my landing. My outstretched left hand caught the hard sand first, absorbing the full weight of my body. If you've ever stomped on an aluminum can and felt it crush unevenly under your foot, you've experienced a sensation similar to my radius and wrist bones compacting under the pressure.

Our holiday weekend at the beach was over.

Next came an overnight stay in the hospital, three surgeries over four years, plates, pins, rods, and physical therapy. Needless to say, the experience was painful. But I like to say it was all worth it. Not for the thrill of skimboarding. Trust me, I'm not that crazy. But for a much better reason.

The first day after returning home from the emergency overnight stay in the hospital, I was heavily medicated. Basically confined to my bed, I drifted in and out of sleep as my arm, throbbing constantly inside a large cast, rested across a pillow on my stomach. At some point that afternoon, my eyes opened to see my son enter the room carrying a blanket and a pillow. Without saying a word, Hampton made a bed for himself on the floor at the foot of my bed and took a nap. Seeing my son's simple act of love and concern for his dad suddenly made all the pain worth it. I smiled for the first time since our day on the beach, pushing a tear from the corner of my eye, and went back to sleep.

It occurred to me later that I had been given a very small glimpse of how Jesus must feel every time a person comes to faith in him. On the cross, he suffered willingly through unimaginable pain, agony, and humiliation. He experienced an excruciating death on our behalf. And I believe whenever someone accepts his sacrifice of love and receives the gift of eternal life, Jesus smiles, and says, "It was worth it."

~ *Greg M. Dodd*

3
Simply Brilliant

I kneeled on my living room floor, crumpled in despair. Quiet tears flowed as I buried my face in my hands. In my heart, I cried out to God for relief. Lost in my sadness, I never heard her walk into the room. I only felt her little hand rest on my shoulder.

"Mommy, what's wrong?" Carolyn asked me in her gentle, four-year-old voice.

I looked up at her inquisitive face that was now leaning close to mine, and I wiped my tears away, trying to construct the right response. I made a weak attempt to smile and reached up to stroke her cheek. I was buying time, but also mesmerized by her innocence.

How could I tell my young daughter all that was wrong? How could I tell her that I felt like a failure as a mom, that her dad was working long, grueling hours and I missed him, and that I feared I was falling into an abyss of depression? How could I tell her all that was ripping at my heart?

I couldn't. So I sighed and whispered a prayer in my heart. *Tell me what to say, Lord. What do I tell her that will satisfy her curiosity without saying too much, and yet still be true?* I shook my head and simply said, "My heart is broken, honey."

She looked me in the eyes, and then a smile began to creep across her face. I hadn't expected that reaction. I looked deeper into her eyes, confused by her joy, but then it seemed clear to me that a brilliant thought had just come to her. She stood up tall and said, "Why don't you just ask Jesus into your heart. I did, and he gave me a new one."

I couldn't help but laugh at the simple reasoning of my child, standing proudly before me. I shook my head as I laughed. *If only it were that simple.* But then again, perhaps it was.

Perhaps it wasn't only simple, but brilliant. Simply brilliant.

When I'd accepted Jesus as my Lord and Savior many years ago, God had indeed given me a brand new heart. He'd given me a heart that could bear everything this life could throw at me, because it was a heart overflowing with the Spirit of God — the Spirit that raised Jesus from the dead. He'd not left me to face trying times with only my strength. He'd given me power from on high. And in my moment of need, he'd sent a child, my sweet Carolyn, to remind me of that strengthening truth.

I pulled Carolyn into my arms and laughed with her, spilling tears of relief where moments earlier, I'd spilled only tears of anguish. I covered her in kisses as she laughed, and I felt alive again with peace and hope.

All because two thousand years ago, God sent his beloved Son into the world to offer us salvation, and two seconds earlier, my sweet Carolyn had come and offered me hope — hope that doesn't disappoint.

I think maybe God did give me a brand new heart that day, and a memory that would hold me up through the toughest times of my life.

- Jean Wilund

# 4
Listen and Hear

My grandson, Mason, was four years old when he and his family were at the beach for the weekend. They had spent all day splashing on water slides and playing in parks. Then they returned to the hotel to shower and get ready for dinner.

His mother called Mason but he did not come. She called him again but still no answer. Then for the third time, she called him in a loud voice, intending to strike fear in him. "Mason Allen McKeithan, you come here right this minute!"

He peeked around the corner of the bedroom door with the Gideon Bible pressed tightly against his ear. "Here I am, Mommy. Whatcha want?"

At first she didn't notice the Bible, but concentrated on his clothes, looking to see if he was ready to go out to dinner. Then she saw it! And in her sweetest, gentlest voice asked, "Mason, what are you doing, honey?"

"Mommy, you told me that God talks to us through the Bible. I was just trying to hear what he wants to tell me."

There is a Bible story in 1 Samuel 2:9 about another little boy who said, "Speak, Lord, your servant is listening." Because Samuel was listening for God's voice, he received an important message to tell Eli the Priest.

Mason has always been a happy child, full of love and laughter. After I leave his company, I feel like smiling the rest of the day about things he said and did. His good humor and sweet spirit are major influences as he touches the lives of others.

Today Mason is fourteen years old and he still wants to hear what God has to tell him. He enjoys hunting and fishing with his dad and his brother. His favorite place to be on Sunday is with his youth group in Bible study and he is active in The Fellowship of Christian Athletes at school. Work ethic is no problem with Mason. He will tackle any job no matter how big and give it his best. When he takes his position as center on his football team, you can be sure he is saying a prayer that win or lose, they will honor Christ in all they do.

Mason has been listening to God speak since he was four years old. His life is proof of the power of the Word in the life of a young child.

We teach the young ones that God speaks through his Word, and we tell them stories about Bible characters like Samuel. How precious when our children believe and in turn, teach it to us adults all over again.

~ Ann Knowles

5
The Legend of the Weeping Willow

Once upon a time, a long time ago, there was a Sunshine Willow. He was always happy and his branches went straight up.

Fox came walking along and said, "Sunshine Willow, why do you look so queer? Why are your branches straight up like grass in the meadow?"

Sunshine Willow said, "I'm always happy so that's why it's like that."

Fox said, "Oh, I won't listen to your silly talk. It looks so queer. I'm going to the river to get some fish. Goodbye."

Then Dog came walking along and asked the Sunshine Willow the same question. Dog walked away and returned to his master.

Sunshine Willow said, "This is very queer. Fox and Dog are usually so kind. Here comes Cat walking along. Maybe she can help me. She is very wise."

Cat walked to Sunshine Willow and said, "Oh my! You look very different today."

Sunshine Willow said, "I do not. I always look like this. What are you talking about?"

Cat went back to her house for her bowl of milk.

Sunshine Willow was very confused that night. The next morning he was very tired and his branches were hanging down.

Wind said, "Oh my! Sunshine Willow, why are your branches weeping down?"

Sunshine Willow said, "I am sad because my friends are making fun of me."

River spoke and said, "Don't worry. You'll be fine. God likes you the way you are. It doesn't matter if you are always happy. It doesn't matter, either, if your branches are always weeping down. It matters how your heart is."

That's the legend of the Weeping Willow.

Moral: It doesn't matter if you're not perfect, God will always love you.

~ Felicity Younts (age 7)

6

A Battle with the Mouse King

Thinking back, I couldn't recall too many difficulties in teaching a two-year-old to stay in her own bed. But every single night I was tucked away in the grandmother room in my first grandchild's home, Hayden crept to my door and turned the door handle.

Even after — in my bed — I read at least two books, flossed teeth, let her sing along to a YouTube video of Matt Redman singing "10,000 Reasons (Bless the Lord)" and then transferred her to her bed to sing a couple of other songs like "Jesus Loves Me" and "Do Your Ears Hang Low," talked about the favorite part of her day and the worst part of her day, gathered all of her stuffed animals into her bed's pillow corral, then said a prayer — ending with Je t'aime ("I love you" in French) and "Sleep tight, don't let the bed bugs bite" — the child was determined to sneak back into my bed for the night. "I want to sleep in your bed, Lovie!"

Trying my best to obey parental rules, every time she opened my door, I sent her back to her own bed. Once, she opened the door so silently I didn't hear her because I was working on my computer. When I finally looked up to see her standing in the doorway with a determined look on her face, she said, "Lovie, you need to go to sleep!" Chastised by a two-year-old, I wondered why she thought I needed to go to sleep. I had work to do. *She* needed to go to sleep! What a challenge it was to get her down for the night.

Later, it would finally dawn on me that if I was asleep, I couldn't hear her sneak into the room to crawl into my bed to have an all night snuggle bunny. Quite the crafty one!

One night, after Hayden had come back into my room because she needed to put on her lips (ChapStick), then come again to potty, then come again to _____ (you fill in the blank with any of ten thousand reasons), I decided to put my grandmother foot down. She had come to my room the last and final time.

However, the look on her face was so troubled, she looked so bereft, with such a waif-in-need-of-love crinkled up look on her bitty brow, that I couldn't bear it when she said, "Lovie, I'm sad."

With that, my heart melted, and my arms opened wide as she rushed to my bedside with the ever-present Honey Bunny I'd given her when she was born — the same bunny she couldn't sleep without. The same bunny we searched the house for every night and naptime so she could drift off into bunny-sleeping-land so there would be no wailing or mourning in Beulah Land.

Putting down the book I was reading, I said, "Precious, why are you sad?" She'd now just turned three. What could have this child so depressed? Could someone be bullying her in pre-school or did she have the entire world's weight on her shoulders? Had she seen something violent on television?

While picking at her Honey Bunny, worrying the one thread that hung down from Honey Bun's well-washed but now ragged looking satin trim, Hayden rushed out, "I want to be in *The Nutcracker* like my Mommie was when she was a little girl!"

Thank the Lord! Something I could fix. She'd seen the photos of her mother and me after a Nutcracker performance and she longed to be like her Mommie. "Honey, don't you worry," I assured her. "We can make that happen." She had just begun to take dance lessons and by the time she was old enough, she would be an easy shoo-in for local Nutcracker performances. Tiny dancers were always in demand.

"But Lovie," Hayden continued with eyes big as hoot owl's, "I'm scared."

"Scared?" I said. "What are you afraid of? It's only a dance performance, Sweetheart. Like a play. Make believe."

Hayden gave Honey Bunny's string a couple more quick pulls before she could at last bare her troubled soul. If possible, her eyes grew even bigger. "Lovie, I'm afraid of mice."

I choked back my laughter, not wanting to make light of her fears. Even I was afraid of a rat. It finally dawned on me that Hayden might have seen *The Nutcracker* performance on television during the Christmas holidays. And there was that ferocious battle with the Nutcracker Prince and the Mouse King when the toys came to life. Ahhhh. And there was that larger than life — to a little girl — Mouse King Christmas decoration that I'd given her mother when she was a child that helped decorate their living room during the holidays. Now all this sadness and worry was making sense.

"You don't have to be sad or afraid. Your Mommie was a mouse one year in The Nutcracker. It's all pretend. Just a show. So you don't have a thing to worry about. You can even be one of the mice yourself. You only wear a mouse costume. You don't really become a mouse. There's nothing to be afraid of. Those are fake swords and no one ever gets hurt."

She didn't miss a beat. "Lovie, can you come tuck me in?"

"Absolutely. Lovie will come tuck you in." Again.

In her bed Hayden said, "I want you to snuggle with me all night long. Never leave me. Let's snuggle all night."

I thought about how unfair it might seem that her mother had her dad to snuggle with all night long. All Hayden had was stuffed animals, her books, and her Bumble Bee flashlight I'd given her for Christmas so she could find missing dolls in the dark, her favorite blanket her Grandmother Cee-Cee and PaPa had given her, and of course, Honey Bunny.

I whispered, "You know Hayden, when you are afraid and scared, you can always talk to God. He's always listening."

"But where is God? How can he hear us?"

Sleepy now, I hadn't counted on theological questions of this magnitude. Keep it simple, I thought. She's so young, keep it simple.

I said, "Well, Precious, God lives in heaven. And he sent his son Jesus to be with us for awhile." She's too young, I thought. I can't give her details yet. Even her mother feels uncomfortable when a picture of Jesus on the cross flashes onto the big screen in church. What happened to Jesus is so unbearable. Oh God, I can't share that with her yet.

That's when Hayden finished my answer for me, "Lovie, Jesus lives in our heart."

Relieved, I said, "That's right Baby Girl. Jesus lives in our heart. And he promises to never leave us. Ever. He snuggles with us always. And you can talk to Jesus too when you're afraid because he's always with you and hears you every time you call."

With that last thought in her head, her fingers finally stopped pulling at Honey Bunny's loose string. Her body relaxed, jerked once, then the child finally drifted off into sandman land.

Later, after feeling a knee stab to my ribs, I sneaked back into my bed and turned out the light, but not before I fluffed up the pillow that rested in Hayden's spot, for I knew snuggle bunnies were made to snuggle and would come hopping back to the nest when the moon was high and the stars were at their shiniest and most sparkly.

In fact, I could count on Hayden's and Honey Bunny's return, especially after I'd been so easily duped. This child wasn't afraid of anything, much less a mouse. She had an imagination that was bigger than the Pacific Ocean and her parents had shared the many ways they had been duped by this intelligent child before. So I fluffed up her pillow and waited for her and Honey Bunny to pay me another nocturnal visit.

I didn't have to wait long before I heard my door handle turn. "Haaaayyyyydennnn," I said before the child cut me off.

"But...Lovie..."

"Hayden, you and Honey Bunny come get in this bed right now." I patted the other side of the mattress. "I saved your spot. It's time to snuggle aaallllll night."

Once safe in my arms, I whispered, "Je t'aime and Goodnight" and once again, her world was made right and she and her Lovie snuggled all night with Honey Bun.

But what would our defense be later when answering to her mom and dad about the broken rules? I could hear my excuses now: "Honey, remember that time you came to my room when you were five years old with every stuffed animal and baby doll you could carry because you could hear the frogs down at the pond and the cicadas and hoot owls outside your open window and you cried, 'The screaming eagles are going to carry off my babies!'?"

I would say, "Well, kids, last night your daughter and I battled the Mouse King. She was simply fearless."

That was my story, and I was sticking to it because time is short. And there will come a time when my Grands won't want to sleep in their Lovie's bed. So for now, I'm going to get in all the snuggles I can because grandmothers need snuggle bunny snuggles too!

- Vicki H. Moss

7
The Runaway

Lights flashing, the police cruiser pulled beside me. The officer signaled through the window to pull over and stop. The gig was up. I was caught. I pulled over to the side of the road, braked, and put the kickstand down on my bicycle (not that I needed it...my little bicycle still had training wheels).

A sigh hissed from my lips as I climbed off. I was eight years old, and running away from home. Well, I had been. Evidently I wasn't anymore.

To be honest, I don't really remember why I was running. It could have been due to some bad grades I was scared to show my parents. My father was a teacher and principal in the same school system I attended. To say that good grades and proper behavior were required of me would be understating it considerably. And those bad grades terrified me. I had gotten lazy, hadn't studied, and paid the price.

Then there was my new little brother. For six years I had been an only child, and then this little usurper appeared, taking, from my point of view, all of Mom's and Dad's attention. I was jealous.

On top of it all, my best friend, Susan, had moved away. She was born into our close-knit family twenty-four hours before I was. We grew up living only a block apart in Winston-Salem. Not only were we cousins but we were also best friends. Susan went to my school and we were in the same grade. We spent family holidays and time at the beach together. Now she and her family had moved to Fayetteville.

That's why I decided to go live at the beach. I knew the way, even from where we lived in Winston-Salem. My family had a beach house on Long Beach and we went there several times a year. I loved that place. I always felt more at home at that beach cottage than any other place I knew.

So it was that I had gathered up my accumulated three dollars and change allowance, sneaked some bread and peanut butter into my knapsack, and instead of going to school that morning, headed off for the beach two hundred miles away.

I pedaled for most of the day on my little bicycle with training wheels.

I got as far as Greensboro, twenty-nine miles away, before the passing policeman took an interest in the earnestly pedaling little boy who should have been in school. He picked me up, put my bicycle in the trunk, and drove to the police station to call my parents.

The hour spent waiting for my parents to come dragged past. It was one of the worst hours in my young life. I anticipated hellfire and brimstone, but instead when they arrived, they came with relief and love. I didn't get the punishment I deserved for the worry I'd put them through. Instead I was scooped into loving arms. I doubt at the time I fully appreciated the lessons learned, both in the futility of running away and receiving love instead of the hearty spanking I deserved. But the memories stayed with me, and in time, I did understand.

I especially understood Jonah running away to the sea, and Moses running to the desert. They both ran away, and in both, God used miracles and love to get them back on course.

Unfortunately, that wouldn't be the only time I ran, either from a situation or into a bottle of alcohol, to escape. God has used miracles to get me back on track as well — although I doubt seriously my purpose in this life was as important as Jonah's and Moses.'

It's so much wiser to stop running from the purpose God intends for us and turn our lives over to him. We discover wonderful places his plan can take us.

~ *Kevin Spencer*

Where can I go from your Spirit?
Where can I flee from your presence?
If I go up to the heavens, you are there;
if I make my bed in the depths, you are there.

Psalm 139:7-8 (NIV)

8
Whatcha Doing, Mom?

In his footed pajamas, Will tiptoed quietly down the dimly lit hallway early in the morning before the sun was even up. With tired looking eyes, the little two-and-a-half year old spied me sitting in my chair, next to a small lamp with my Bible open on my lap.

"Whatcha doing, Mom?"

"Praying," I said.

"Are you…are you praying for me?"

With a smile on my face I scooped up my little son and chuckled, "Yes, I'm praying for you."

That was seventeen years ago.

Sometimes as I sit in the same chair, in the same house, I peer down the hall to where my young son once stood, asking if I was praying for him. I hear that sweet voice like it was yesterday.

Today, however, I hear strong, adult voices of Will and his sisters.

The weekly text messages, phone calls, and emails I receive asking me to pray about a college exam, or a sickness, or an important decision, let me know that they witnessed their mother's commitment to pray.

Praying for our children is the single best thing we'll ever do for them. I often think of it like this: If I don't pray for my children, then who will?

Lamentations 2:19 tells us to cry out to God for the life of our children. Many times we see the evidence of answered prayers. But sometimes we never know what our prayers protected our children from or how our prayers changed them.

Our children are a precious gift to us. And our prayers for them are our powerful gift back.

~ *Debbie Presnell*

9
A Land Where Magic Grows

Grandpa Roy's gray head bowed as he led me under a white arch and into a world of wonder. In the seven years I'd been alive, never had my eyes seen anything so amazing as Grandpa's garden. He bent over the green frill of a plant and gave it a tug. A carrot emerged from the earth. Grandpa used the leg of his bibbed overalls to wipe dirt off the carrot, then handed me what I considered to be a miracle. That simple act, plus the splendor of a marigold-fringed plot of land where magic happened, planted a seed of longing in my heart.

A month later, a package from Grandma arrived in the mail. Inside was a golden-edged book that taught how to garden. The front cover had a hole in it large enough to expose a package of seeds. Pictures showed how the life inside a seed breaks out of its shell and then burrows through the soil in search of sunlight.

That year I became a gardener, a tiller of soil, the caretaker of plants.

Years later a husband, two sons, and a house where grass got converted into a garden, came into my life. We spent hours in our garden and even more time harvesting then preserving the fruit of our labors. The boys loved taking turns thump-thumping a wooden stomper in a crock filled with shredded cabbage destined to become sauerkraut. We took turns making up stories while packing pickles and had contests to see who could peel an apple in one continuous strand. Those boys grew faster than weeds, moved on to college, marriage and became fathers.

Now a flock of five grandchildren come to visit that same backyard garden. As Grandpa and Grandma we've had the joy of introducing them to the world of plants and insect life. At the age of five, while examining a broccoli plant, Nate watched a butterfly land on a leaf. His hands reached out. The butterfly spun upward and a chase began. Nate's voice sang, "Look Grandma, a flying flower."

Having grandchildren has returned me to my youth. Once again I marvel at how flowers morphed into tomatoes, eggplants, cucumbers, apples and blueberries.

They've called to ask, "Will the raspberries be ripe by the time we come to visit?" How I love to watch them harvest not only berries and peas, but take a walk-about through the rest of garden in search of nourishment. Nourishment, not only for their bellies, but also for their souls. The backyard soil has become a garden planted with laughter, watered with words, fed with love until memories grew, blossomed and even in the cold of winter have fueled conversations.

Around the table we are often asked, "Are these green beans from the garden?" One of them will say, "Remember how Grandma got over one hundred tomatoes from Edith? She was one amazing plant, wasn't she?"

A smile will burrow through memories as I recall the trip to the garden center. The grandchildren and I picked out a Rosemary plant to bring home and take up residence in the section of earth named the memory garden. The grandchildren gathered around. One dug a hole; two of them released Rosemary from her plastic pot. Another grandchild placed Rosemary in the hole. The fifth child covered her roots with soil and I watered her. I told them how Rosemary was a plant of remembrance. Rosemary's roots sank deep. She flavored soup, filled the air with fragrance and stood as a reminder of Grandpa Roy, Grandma, my husband, sons and grandchildren. To this day, the aroma of a love that spans generations continues to spread on a plot of land in our own backyard.

~ *Susan Engebrecht*

10

Mommy, You Stop It!

One day, it all finally caught up with me — and what a horrible day it was. I sat in the middle of the kitchen floor, crying huge tears, blubbering and shuddering like a child whose dreams had just been crushed.

I had been a single mom for four years, and we had done all right. I was working full time and managed to scrape by week after week on a secretary's salary, making way for the occasional small toy or ice cream cone or secondhand doll or frilly dress for my little princess. I was careful with my money, only buying what we really needed, shopping for all our clothes at thrift stores and yard sales.

Of course, just like any hardworking mama with a little cash in her pocket, I was guilty every now and then of being not so frugal — like the times we ate out or ordered pizza or rented movies. Nevertheless, I was still as careful as I could be, paying what I could on the utility bills, the daycare bill, the car payment, the rent, and the miscellaneous groceries, laundry, and household things that came along. Then there were the baby and wedding showers, birthday parties, and holiday gifts to contend with.

Until that day, we had eked by. We'd never starved or gone without clothing or electricity, but things had changed. Now, I was wondering whether or not the heat would still be on in a couple weeks. Would we even have a home to heat? Would they repossess my car or boot my daughter out of preschool?

Where would I get the ten dollars for Cissy's school photos by Tuesday? Which of the five cans of vegetables should I open to go with the last package of hotdogs for dinner? And how in the world was I going to buy anyone a single thing for Christmas, only a few weeks away? My heart broke at the thought of my precious daughter sleepily walking down the stairs in her footed pajamas on Christmas morning, only to find nothing under our lonely little tree that sat in the corner of our tiny living room.

The landlord had stopped by just a few minutes earlier, asking about the rent that was now five days late. I had known I'd have to pay it late, just as I had done with my car payment the week before. As soon as he walked away, I closed the front door, took a deep breath, ran into the kitchen in that nervous panic people get when they want to get away but have no place to go, and I collapsed onto the cold linoleum. I sat there in a crossed-leg, hunched-over heap, holding my face in my hands and bawling uncontrollably until my little girl came stumbling into the kitchen, lured away from her cartoons by her concern for her sobbing mommy. Cissy was only four years old and smart for her age, but she had never been the sentimental, cuddling mommy's girl some children are, so I was surprised when she ran in to check on me.

As adults, we often have the impression that we can never break down in front of our children, but must have it all together all the time. In our attempt to shelter them from all the evil and ugly and scary things in the world, we try to maintain our composure under all circumstances. This time, I just couldn't do that.

As I looked at my child, I thought of the times God had sent people in my life to help me out of trouble, especially since I'd become a mother. My grandparents, some of the most amazing people I know, had surprised me with a new refrigerator when mine broke down and gave me money to buy some groceries to put into it.

Another time, folks from church secretly placed several Christmas gifts in my car while I sat inside, unaware of their kindness. A family friend graciously and thoughtfully took my daughter shopping at Christmastime and brought the happy three-year-old home with gifts she picked out for me all by herself, including a Cookie Monster soap dispenser that didn't at all match my bathroom but quickly became my favorite accessory at the sink.

People at Stan's Tire Center gave me extra days to come up with money for a needed tire. Others have given me bags and boxes of hand-me-down clothes for my daughter. My uncles spent hours under the hood of my old minivan to keep it running for another day. The Board of Deacons at my church helped me pay for expensive dental work I desperately needed but couldn't afford.

Yes, many times in my life God has sent people, who I like to think of as angels. Then, in my moment of weakness and defeat, I believe he sent that barefoot, chocolate-faced, curly-haired cherub rushing into the kitchen.

As I sat there sobbing and shuddering, still shaken by the landlord's visit, my mind scrambling for any way to make a few extra dollars quickly, my little girl gave me a hug and said, "Mommy, you stop it. God will take care of us."

She said it sternly, with all the oomph of any preacher I'd ever heard, and she pointed one finger at me while placing the other hand on her hip, just as she had seen me do to her a thousand times. She may as well have thrown a brick at me, because it hit me that hard.

Guilt washed over me. Had I spent time nurturing her, teaching her to pray when she was sad, sick, frightened, or worried, only to throw my own advice aside when I need it most? Had I forgotten that God promised to meet our needs and proved that to me over and over again through all the angels and miracles he'd sent into my life at just the right moment?

After hugs from my child, I took her advice. I stopped it. We sat on the kitchen floor that night praying to God who would take care of us. And as he'd done in the past, he has continued to do that ever since!

Now, whenever I feel like life is too much to bear, I remember my stern young angel reminding me, "Mommy, you stop it. God will take care of us."

- Autumn Conley

11
Art of Communicating

With four growing children and no nearby relatives, I felt the maxim, "The family that prays together stays together," was a truism worth practicing. Especially since the day in October when our pastor visited and began making conversation with our 2 ½ year old. She was playing with toy animals.

"Which do you like best?" he inquired.

"Wino," she replied immediately.

Hastily, I explained that wino in baby talk is short for rhino, short for rhinoceros.

Later in the conversation she intimated she also liked "booze."

That one was not so easy to explain. My older children had been designing invitations for a Halloween party and had drawn many scary ghouls, ghosts, witches and goblins. The "Boos!" had flown fast and furious! After the initial frights, the little one had become fascinated with the scary creatures and would bring pencil and paper to her sisters and brother to "make boos."

The pastor said he understood and did not believe we were running an illegal still but it's rather hard for me to believe that "revenoor" was really walking in our patch of woods a few days later as a part of his daily constitutional!

It is certainly understandable why the good Lord gave us a day when the only work we do is absolutely necessary. But I don't think we did it the way he intended.

My Sunday school teacher made the remark, "I don't understand people who ask, "What's good about it?" when you say, "Good morning."

Fortunately, my family wasn't in the room when she made the statement and if she couldn't tell by looking at me, just why mornings are a bad time for some people, I wasn't about to tell her.

Perhaps she thought I was awake just because my eyes were open. Not so! It's just that when I inadvertently sprayed my hair with spray starch, some of it got on my eyelids and they wouldn't close.

I never contributed anything orally to the class because I imagined that if I opened my mouth, little blue bubbles would rise to the ceiling and pop. I don't think they should put Head & Shoulders in tubes that look like toothpaste.

"How do you do it?" some people asked, curious how I managed to get four children ready for Sunday school, particularly since my husband's job at the Federal Prison required a schedule change every three months. One quarter he worked days, the next evenings, followed by night, then the cycle would repeat.

"Oh," I smiled and talked between my teeth, holding back the bubble, "Everybody helps."

The children could tell how they helped much better than I. Like the morning David wore his pants backwards to church. Or the time, Lisa bent over for something and we discovered she was wearing the bottoms of her pink and white flowered baby-doll pajamas.

Then there was the time the nursery workers were concerned when Cindy was just a little thing.

"She fussed a lot this morning," they told me. "That's unusual for her."

It was not until I was undressing her at home that I discovered the crumpled tissue paper in the toes of her new shoes.

Then there was the time Lisa informed us that a boy in her class at school learns "kittycasm" at his church and why don't we.

And once Lori had been shown a picture of Jesus knocking on a door, and wanted to know why he was knocking. "That's symbolic," I explained. "Jesus knocks on our heart's door because he wants to come in and live with us." "Oh," she replied, "so that's why we hear that thump-thump-thump."

Every time we observed The Lord's Supper, there were explanations and our saying, "No, you cannot partake, because you're not a Christian."

"Then I want to be a Christian!" our then-six-year-old announced.

"Do you want to be a Christian so you can have grape juice and crackers?" I asked.

"No, she replied seriously. "I'd rather have peanut butter and bread."

About that time, we decided upon more rigorous religious training at home. During our attempts at family worship, they at least began thinking for themselves.

Lori and Lisa were sitting on the couch, looking at a Bible Story book.

"I know why God didn't want Adam and Eve to eat them apples," Lisa said.

Lori, the oldest, replied, "Well, so do I."

"Yeah," Lisa said agreeably. "It's because they had them snake germs on 'em."

As the children grew older, they sometimes read the Bible stories to our family gatherings. After reading, the one in charge got to ask questions relating to the reading.

Lisa explained that she was going to read about Abraham and Isaac from the book of Genesis.

After finishing her story, she asked, "Where did I get the story I read?" hoping for the answer, "Genesis."

Cindy, the youngest one, raised her hand, was called upon, and answered confidently, "From the Bible."

They were forever looking for chances to stump Mom and Dad. One Sunday evening Lisa came out of her class with a paper. On it was written a memory verse.

"What does this say?" she asked.

"Ecclesiastes 3:11," I replied.

"Do you know who wrote Ecclesiastes?" she asked.

Wracking my brain, I was trying desperately to remember. Moses? Solomon? Uncertain, and feeling quite inadequate, I had to give up.

Her entire countenance brightened as she answered, "Mrs. Palmer wrote Ecclesiastes. And I wrote the other words."

Hmmmm.

We parents never get the last word. They have an answer for everything. Later, I had just finished washing dishes and was mopping the floor. Cindy came to the doorway about to step inside. Just as I opened my mouth to protest she asserted, "Mommy, every time I'm hungry, you start mopping."

Her dad told her to stay out of the top drawer of the filing cabinet, explaining, "You might upset it."

"I can't," she replied. "It doesn't have a stomach."

Their logic is simply not to be understood. One night, when Cindy was five years old, she'd been told several times, "Go to bed!"

She began to wail, "I want to watch that TV show."

Her dad said, "I cooked you two egg sandwiches, you had two glasses of lemonade, one glass of orange juice, now what you should do is say "Thank you" and go to bed."

She yelled, "Thaaank yoooou!" Then stalking down the hallway, asserted huffily, "That's the last time I'm ever letting you do anything for me."

- Yvonne Lehman

12
All God's Children

All children are special. I believe that. When our granddaughter, Addie Grace, came into our lives, she brought that message in ways we never anticipated. She came earlier than expected, weighing less than expected and with some unexpected attributes. Addie Grace was born with a rare chromosome deficiency that rendered her virtually deaf and would cause her to be developmentally delayed and mentally deficient.

The early days of her life presented challenges for her and for all of us as we sought to process what this meant for her and particularly for her mom and dad. She was their first child and they were unprepared for what this would mean in their lives. Their experience was like that of any new parents — full of sleepless nights, imagined and unimagined fears, and the day-by-day learning to care for a helpless baby. Yet beyond these ordinary experiences were many days of doctor's visits, tests, therapies, and consultations that led to surgeries and hospital stays.

"What do you think caused this?" I asked my daughter one day.

"God caused it. He made her this way." Matter-of-fact words of acceptance.

I dared not ask her nor myself the question lingering on my heart — the question any relative of a special needs child may want to know. I had learned God's answers to unasked questions come in many ways and in his time.

As we watched Addie Grace grow and bring blessing to our lives, we could see some of his answers unfolding. We took extra joy in each milestone she accomplished — pushing up, rolling over, crawling and finally walking at age eight. We witnessed how she learned to recognize her favorite places and respond to pictures of objects or people.

One of the most precious things she began doing was a special way of greeting. She started one day by approaching her paternal grandmother and laying her head on her lap waiting for Mimi, as she was called, to pat her head or rub her back. Her parents called it "Mimi love" because at first she seemed to restrict the act to Mimi alone.

When we came to visit, however, one of the first things she did was to come to me and lay her head on my lap. I felt special to receive "Mimi love."

Soon she began expressing this show of affection to others — sometimes approaching older women at the grocery or in the mall to show "Mimi love." They must have sensed she was a special child, for no one rebuffed her. Her gesture was a particular blessing to the heart of a 104-year-old family friend who prays for Addie daily. When Addie was taken for a visit, she went right to the dear lady and laid her head on her lap.

Our daughter has become accustomed to various reactions of people in public places when they see Addie Grace. They wonder why she doesn't speak when they say "hello" or why she chews on a special plastic tube to keep her occupied or why she makes strange sounds instead of words.

In one encounter a curious little girl asked what was wrong with Addie. Our daughter answered that God had created her the way she is. This caused the small inquisitor to pose the question of whether Addie could walk or talk. "She can walk, but she can't talk," was the response.

The little girl remarked, "She's beautiful, but I feel sorry for her."

Our daughter assured her she shouldn't feel that way because God had made Addie. This prompted the deeper question many people think, but are reluctant to ask, "*Why* did God make her that way?"

"That's a very good question," came the reply.

With wisdom only God can give, the little girl reflected, then said, "Maybe it's so I don't have to feel sorry for myself — I can walk and talk."

Fighting tears, our daughter told her, "That's a perfect answer."

It's true, just as the psalmist wrote in Psalm 100:3 (NKJV). *Know that the LORD, He is God; It is He who has made us, and not we ourselves; we are His people and the sheep of His pasture.*

God's ways and purposes are sometimes past our finding out, but we can trust him and thank him for his providence in creating all his children

We especially thank him for blessing us with a sweet lamb, Addie Grace, and the joyful moments she brings to our lives.

~ Sandra Fischer

13
Uninvited Visitor

During a sleepless night, my thoughts traveled to a distant time and land and my long-forgotten childhood in Eurajoki, Finland. The thoughts were so persistent that it seemed it was the time to revisit the memories, whether I wanted to or not.

There I sat in a large "*tupa,*" a family room type kitchen, watching Mother make my favorite meal, mashed potatoes and brown gravy with slivers of fried pork in it. The smells filled my senses, but that day they held no joyful expectation for me.

I kept glancing at my little brother Tauno, who lay on a colorful rag rug on the floor trying to play with some wooden blocks. He hadn't eaten all day and with his blue eyes shining feverishly he didn't look well. Tauno wasn't one to complain, but he had earlier said that his belly was sore.

Some of us children had a cold, with runny noses and cough, so it seemed that Tauno had caught it also. Still I felt uneasy as recent sad memories flooded my mind:

> I saw our old green cradle, decorated with hand-painted roses on the headboard and footboard, being carried away empty by one of our older brothers. I had understood from the hushed tones of grownups that something sad and fearful was taking place.
>
> My little sister Elvi, who to me had always looked like an angel with her curly blond ringlets and her porcelain skin, was dying of meningitis. Earlier she had been moved away from the *tupa* to a small room across the hall because our parents had been worried that others in our large family would catch it.
>
> What meningitis was, I did not fully understand. But, I knew from stories about my own infancy that I also had had it, and only a divine miracle had saved me from death. Now my little sister was in its mortal grip... Mother and Father were with baby Elvi, and then later the old country doctor came and went.

I had periodically sneaked to peek though the keyhole to see what was happening behind that ominous closed door. Now I saw Mother bent over, washing Elvi tenderly in the small washbasin with a white washcloth. I saw tears running down her pale face and falling on the baby. Mother's pretty brown hair was coming loose from the usual tight braid.

I had burst into tears and had run to my room and my bed to comfort Tauno, who was as confused with the events as was I. Somehow I hoped that baby Elvi would get well, because she was bathed and Mother had dressed her in a pretty white dress with a pink pinafore. But deep down in my almost six-year-old mind and heart, I had sensed that Elvi was gone.

I remembered solemn people coming to our farm in dark clothing. Tauno and I were left behind at home in care of some elderly woman, as the rest of the family and relatives exited the farmhouse with the little corpse that had been our angel sister. Tauno and I whispered wordless farewell.

Now, I was afraid again as I watched Tauno looking so sick. Our parents must have sensed that something other than a common cold was wrong with him, because right after dinner, which was eaten almost in silence, Father prepared the horse and buggy. Both parents rode off with Tauno as I pressed my face against the cold windowpane trying to see them as long as possible.

Tauno was taken to the hospital in Rauma, a coastal town about an hour ride with the buggy from our home. It seemed that my parents were gone for days. Iili-Mummo, our diminutive, stooped grandma was watching us children; while an odd silence engulfed our usually rowdy family.

I was waiting anxiously for Tauno's return. I saved a pretty emptied Johanna-coffee cardboard box for him under my bed for a homecoming present. Finally the horse and buggy arrived, but only my parents were in it.

My world seemed to end as I was told matter-of-factly by emotionless-looking parents that Tauno had died of ruptured appendix. Death had cruelly visited us uninvited again.

I heard from bits and pieces of adult conversations that Tauno had said shortly before his death that baby Elvi had come to take him to heaven.

I felt comfortless. I crawled under my bed, and I did not want to be part of life. Tauno and I had shared a bed. Fear became my unwanted bedfellow for years to come.

I remembered Tauno's funeral day, ironically the most brilliant summer day with a mild breeze and birds singing in the nearby tall evergreen trees.

We all gathered around a deep dark grave, and the smell of fresh turned soil was in the air. The minister said some words, and a hymn was sung. Then, some men started to lower a small casket where I knew Tauno was, and people started to throw handfuls of soil on it.

I panicked, but I could not get the words out. Finally I screamed. "Don't put my brother in the grave! Don't cover him with dirt! He can't breathe under there!"

That summer I often saw Father walking in silence, looking at the growing crops. Mother was sullen and pale.

My being was lifeless, like a spent flower with all sap and freshness gone. I felt only coldness, even in my sleep. Tauno and I had slept with our heads at opposite ends of our shared bed, feet touching, often giggling and tickling each other's feet. Now my feet only felt the cold lifeless sheets.

I tried to remember his voice, the pretty little song he liked to sing — "*On lautalla pienoinen kahvila, aalloilla seilaava.*" (About a tiny cafeteria on a ferryboat, sailing on the waves.)

I so desperately wanted to remember the times when we had gone together to check on the neighbor's bull in its fenced pasture, thinking how excitingly scary it was; the times when we had played by the river, placing bark ships to sail to mysterious faraway places; the times when we had played games running alongside Siti, our Fathers prize horse, sometimes even running between its long legs, a foolish and dangerous game; the times when we had sat on our large boulder and watched the pretty lambs gracing the field, the lazy river flowing by.

We even once tried to sell sheep droppings in a paper bag as licorice to unsuspecting children going to school past our farm (those were country children so they recognized the product unfortunately), and enjoying each other's company.

Now I felt so infinitively alone that even *kollamo,* Mother's barley cakes, could neither delight nor comfort me. Fear followed me everywhere. I saw death in every shadow mocking me. I could not go to the outhouse by myself. I would rather have held on forever or made in my undies, so I was allowed to use potty inside the house again at the age of six.

I had four older sisters, but I had not bonded much with them. Tauno and baby Elvi had been my life and love, as long as I could remember. The older sisters were already in school and they had homework and chores to do when home.

I struggled to remember how Elvi and Tauno looked. Over time, their features became faded, like a garment left too long outside on the clothes line to dry. Even that small comfort was stolen from me without my permission.

Aili, one of my sisters liked to tell stories, so I clung to her. Her stories were a better place than my reality. They carried me away from my drowning sadness and the suffocating fear.

My parents' genteel world had started to come apart, when in World War II Russia had taken the Karelian Isthmus. Mother and Father had lost their large ancestral country lakefront estate with its island, abundant fields, and forests. They had been living in a small coastal lowland farmstead that the government had given as a resettlement to them, where frost and floods (now even death) were seasonal visitors, giving them only a meager harvest.

Father had been with some local carpenters building our farmhouse. It would never be fully finished or painted. Life was changed for us all.

Evenings I sometimes heard Mother and Father reminiscing of Karelia, dreaming of a place and time lost forever.

I escaped more and more into imaginary world of dreams, stories and later books, where I was safe. That helped me forget some of the grief and think about the good childhood times.

Weathered Old House

Weathered old house
Wooden, part yellow, part blue
It stands slanted
On the edge of small hill
Alone and so very still

Ancient pine trees,
Bold, some burly, some tall
They whisper the secrets
Of many bygone years
The blissful laughter, the salty tears

Young fluffy lambs
Shy, some black, some white
They graze the fields of the house
Walk in the sands of the river gone dry
Never wondering why

Stooped thin woman,
Hair, some white, some gray
She gazes the vistas,
The house on the hill
Memories of bygone years vivid still.

Laughing bare footed children,
Garments, some yellow, some blue
They danced on the fields
They played near the sheep,
In sands of the river flowing through.

The wayfaring woman
Eyes part teary, part dry
She gazes the vistas
The house on the hill
The tired wind gone almost still

Ancient pine trees
Bold, some burly, some tall
They whisper the secrets
Of many bygone years
The blissful laughter, the salty tears

~ Mirjam Budarz

14
The Accident

My bike is too little for me, Andy said.
"I will sneak my sister's big bike out for a ride."

Andy felt like a really big boy on the ten-speed bike
so he rode up and down streets for a long time.

Then he decided to ride up a big hill.

Andy came zooming down the hill in a zig-zag way.
He hit a rock and Andy went flying off the bike.

Andy landed in the road and a car was coming.
Andy was unconscious. The car stopped.

The man and woman in the car asked a neighbor boy who Andy was.
They took Andy home and Andy's parents took him to the Emergency Center.

Andy's head was bleeding.
The ambulance, with its siren blaring loudly, rushed Andy to the hospital.

A special doctor was called and X-rays were made of Andy's head.
He had a concussion.
Andy's parents asked Christians to pray for him.

Andy was in the hospital for three days.
He couldn't eat much the first two days because he felt sick.
He had many cuts, bruises and scratches and a bone in his head was cracked,
but the doctor said he would get well.

Andy said he wouldn't ride his sister's bike again until he was bigger.
While he was getting well at home he lay on the couch,
watched television and ate everything he could find.

When he was better Andy went to church to thank God for helping him
get better and thank the people for praying for him.

- David Andrew Lehman (age 9)

15

Walking, Fixing, and Transforming

Walking in Daddy's Shoes

Drew, my two-year-old grandson, wobbled into the living room with his daddy's size eleven gray Nikes on his small feet. I watched as Drew held up his short arms for balance while his toothpick-looking legs shuffled one large shoe in front of the other. Beneath his blonde curls, his smiling face said, "Look at me, I'm walking in my Daddy's shoes."

Like many small boys, Drew wants to walk like his Daddy walks, talk like his Daddy talks, and mimic his every action. My son, Eric, watched Drew struggle, stumble and almost fall as he made his way across the room. But Eric never took his eyes off of Drew. He was ready to catch him if he fell. Drew finished his journey, and stood in front of his proud Daddy where he heard, "Good job, Drew!"

Major decisions, financial concerns, and family problems sometimes leave me feeling like I'm wobbling through life while trying to shuffle through problems that are way too big for me.

Yet, like Drew, I want to walk like my heavenly father walks, talk like he talks, and mimic his every action. I know he is watching as I struggle, stumble, and sometimes almost fall. But he never takes his eyes off me. He is ready to catch me before I fall.

So, I need to put a smile on my face, shuffle along, and focus on my father. Someday, when I complete my journey here on earth, and stand before him, I hope to hear, "Good job!"

DaDa Fix It

"Broke," Drew said as he held up his red Matchbox car in one hand and a set of wheels in another. I watched as a frown furrowed his forehead while he turned the car over and tried to snap the wheels back into place.

With all of the manual dexterity of a two-year-old, Drew worked to replace the wheels on the underside of his small car. But it soon became evident, even to Drew, that this problem was too difficult for him. I expected him to become frustrated, perhaps cry or maybe even throw his toy down, but he walked over and calmly placed it on the coffee table. He looked at Amy, his mama, and said, "DaDa fix it." Drew left his broken car on the table and turned around to play with something else.

"Whenever something breaks," Amy said, "Drew just puts it down and says, 'DaDa fix it.' He thinks his daddy can fix anything."

I have many things in life that I hold up and say, "Broke." Relationships, finances, health — broke. A frown furrows my forehead while I try to put the pieces of my life back together.

With all the spiritual maturity of my fifty-four years, I work to fix my problems until it becomes evident that they are too difficult for me. Unlike Drew, sometimes I do become frustrated, cry, and even throw up my hands in despair.

Yet the Lord tells us to give him our broken pieces; to place them at the foot of the cross, walk away, and have enough faith to say, my Heavenly Father will fix it.

I *know* He can fix anything.

The Ultimate Transformer

"Close your eyes and hold out your hands, Drew. I brought you a surprise."

Three-year-old Drew did a little happy dance, squinched his face so tightly his eyes closed, then stuck out his small arms.

I placed Super Grover in Drew's hands, and stepped back. He opened his eyes and mouth at the same time, and just as quickly his mouth closed and his expression turned into a frown. "What does it do, Nana?"

Before I could answer, Drew said, "It doesn't do anyfing!"

Stuffed Super Grover didn't do one thing. He was clearly a dud as far as Drew was concerned. I soon understood Drew's disappointment. He showed me his favorite new toys, Transformer Rescue Bots. Drew could transform them from robots into rescue vehicles. He had Chase (the police car), Heatwave (the fire engine), Blades (the rescue helicopter), Boulder (the bulldozer), and Optimus Prime, the leader who assigned underground missions designed to protect all mankind.

Super Grover or Rescue Bots?

Now even I could see that Super Grover was a dud.

Jesus stood in the synagogue and read, *"The Spirit of the Lord is on me. He has anointed me to preach good news to the poor…proclaim freedom to the captives and recovery of sight to the blind, set free the oppressed, to proclaim the year of the Lord's favor."* He then declared, *"Today as you listen, this Scripture has been fulfilled."*

The people in Jesus hometown had just been presented with the Ultimate Transformer. But he was clearly a dud as far as they were concerned, so they rejected him, and drove him out of town.

Throughout Jesus' three years of ministry, he drove out evil spirits, healed the sick, fed thousands with only two fish and five loaves of bread, raised the dead, and transformed the lives of everyone who heard and believed. He even died on a cross to save us from our sins.

And his ministry continues even today, two thousand years later. Jesus Christ took me, a broken, insecure little girl, and healed my heart so I could finally laugh, and play, and sing, and become the person he created me to be. Jesus Christ transformed my life, and I'm so thankful that he did.

The Ultimate Transformer will heal the heart and transform the life of anyone who accepts Him as Lord and Savior.

Nothing else can compare.

~ Susan Dollyhigh

16
Food, Fun, and Fireworks

"Look how much Uncle Francis gave me!" I showed my mother a dollar bill.

The first part of July, in the 1950's, was an exciting time for me as a youngster. On the 4th, mother would prepare a picnic lunch for our family and we'd go to a park in a neighboring town, where the firefighters had a yearly nighttime fireworks display. Our seats were blankets on the ground. Each aerial display brought ooh's and aah's from the hundreds of people watching.

That was always fun. But so was the evening when mother's relatives came to our house in the country for family fireworks, watermelon, and hand-cranked homemade ice cream.

A week or so before the 4th of July, an uncle, an aunt, and our grandmother would give my younger brother, O.J., and me money to buy fireworks. We'd each have two or three dollars to spend on sparklers, lady fingers, and Roman candles.

My brother and I could barely contain ourselves on the day we went into town to buy our fireworks. Our first stop was the market. "Come on kids, let's pick out a watermelon. It has to be a Black Diamond. They are the best," Daddy told us. Soon he was thumping the various watermelons to select a ripe one. He had been raised in Oklahoma where his family grew several acres of watermelons to sell, eat, and share with neighbors. "Listen for a hollow sound," he told us. I soon learned how to test for melon ripeness.

Our next stop was the grocery store for mother to get necessary supplies. My parents didn't need to buy much at a store. They grew a large garden with mother canning everything she could. Daddy had a cow that supplied our milk, cream, and butter. Mother raised chickens for eggs and eating. Pigs provided the bacon, pork chops, and ham that we enjoyed.

When we finally came to the fireworks stand, O.J. and I practically pranced around the display. I didn't realize it then, but the adults knew they were giving us practical experience in handling money. We soon filled our grocery sacks. Daddy also bought a few fireworks. He particularly liked to get one or two cherry bombs to set off at the end of our evening.

A stop to get a block of ice finished our morning of shopping.

As we traveled home, the lady fingers came in and out of my sack many times. I hoped my parents would let me shoot some of them before evening.

"Help me get the ice around the watermelon," Daddy said as he placed the large melon in a washtub. O.J. and I scooped up the small pieces of ice that Daddy chipped off the ice block with the ice pick. "Let's get the melon completely covered, so it will be ice cold for eating this evening."

"Do the dusting and then maybe we'll have time for you to light a few of your lady fingers," Mother instructed. The dust flew around the house as I wiped off the tops of everything I could reach.

As the sun started setting in the west, our relatives arrived. "Grandmother, look how many Roman candles I got." O.J. brought out his lady fingers to show Aunt Iva.

"Let's have some watermelon before it gets dark," Daddy announced. Soon O.J. and I were competing to see how far we each could spit watermelon seeds.

Earlier Mother had mixed our own fresh milk and eggs with other ingredients for ice cream and had it waiting to be frozen. The men took turns on the hand-cranked ice cream freezer. "Let me try," I insisted. As the ice and rock salt turned the mixture into ice cream, the crank became harder and harder to turn.

"It's dark now, can we start our fireworks?" O.J. asked.

"Watch me! Watch me!" The sparklers provided a variety of entertainment as O.J. and I made circles, stars, and boxes in the air and watched to see how long the sparkly designs remained. "Write your name," Mother encouraged. Writing my name in the air with a sparkler brought much laughter as I tried this feat.

"This is the last one," I announced as I held a Roman candle in the air. Our private fireworks display was soon over, but the memories are still fun to talk about.

Eating the yummy ice cream ended our evening of family fun. Homemade ice cream remains one of my favorite desserts and I still enjoy viewing a fireworks display. To me, those are precious memories.

~ Helen L. Hoover

17

Only in Our Hearts

During our engagement, Betsy and I talked about having children. It was an exciting topic. We also discussed some possible names. One might think that since my name is Robert Elroy Buck IV, I would push for a namesake, especially after such a heritage. However, that was not what was on my heart.

Betsy and I wanted to begin a Godly heritage. We did not grow up in Christian homes, but each received Jesus into our hearts when in our twenties. We consider ourselves first generation believers.

Before our wedding, in my Bible reading, I was struck by the friendship between Jonathan, King Saul's son who one would expect to inherit the throne, and David, a man destined to become the next king. Jonathan's love for David was unselfish and pure. In fact, while Jonathan was trying to protect David from his father's rage, they made a covenant together because Jonathan loved David as he loved his own soul. First Samuel 20:23 tells us Jonathan said to David, *"As for the agreement of which you and I have spoken, behold, the Lord is between you and me forever."*

What a beautiful picture of sacrificial love, the Lord being between two people. For Betsy and me, and our upcoming life together, I thought of God being between us, protecting our love. How would it change the way we interacted? Wouldn't it encourage us to yield to God's abiding love in us as we loved each other — loving with his love instead of our own self-centered love?

When I told Betsy about it, she loved the thought of God being between us forever. In fact, as a symbol of our desire to have the Lord's love in the center of our relationship, we decided that if we ever had a boy, we would name him Jonathan David.

On the day of our wedding, Betsy surprised me with the inscription "I Sam 20:23" on the inside of my ring.

On February 13, less than two years into marriage, Betsy went into labor with our first child. In was an exciting time, but her labor was very rough. I tried to help with the breathing, but she was in a lot of pain.

Finally, very late in the evening, Betsy was told to push. I held her hand, trying to encourage her as the doctor behind the birth sheet declared the head was crowning. Betsy continued to push, knowing soon she would hold our child in her arms.

Then it happened, from behind the sheet, we heard that our baby was here. With joy, Betsy and I looked at each other in smiling relief waiting to hear whether it was a boy or a girl, but no one said anything.

Our baby was whisked away and attended to in an outer part of the delivery room.

"What did we have?" Betsy called out. "Where's my baby?"

One of the nurses looked our way and said, "It's a boy," but they all continued to work on him. He had been in the birth canal so long, his vitals had dropped to dangerous levels. They were giving him oxygen.

Anxious moments passed, but finally a nurse emerged from the treatment area with our baby, announcing he was fine.

"What's his name?" the nurse asked, handing him to Betsy.

"Jonathan David Buck," I said as Betsy cradled him in her arms.

"Happy Valentine's Day!" the nurse said smiling.

Jonathan was born at 12:04 a.m., the first Valentine's Day baby in the state that year.

Later, as I held Jonathan, I thought of what a fitting Valentine's gift he was; a physical representation of Betsy's and my love for each other.

Jonathan David was a gift directly from the heart of God to us as a couple.

This fragile little guy, with such tiny fingers and toes was totally dependent on us. God had entrusted a little human being to our care. I thought of how dependent Jonathan was and then how dependent I am on my Heavenly Father.

As time went on, I began to see God's love in a whole new way I could not have understood if I were not a father myself.

I thought of John 3:16. *God so loved the world, that he gave his only Son, that whoever believes in him should not perish but have eternal life.*

Would I be willing to give Jonathan up for someone else's sake? Yet God did it for me even when I was against him.

How could God watch his son go through so much pain and suffering? How could he let Jesus go through all that for me?

His love for me does not make sense when I see it from the eyes of an earthly father. This quality of love is beyond my reasoning.

And then there's the quality of love I'm to have for him.

I consider verses like Matthew 10:37. *He who loves father or mother more than me is not worthy of me; and he who loves son or daughter more than me is not worthy of me.* (NASB)

And Luke 14:26: *If anyone come to me and does not hate his own father and mother and wife and children and brothers and sisters, yes, and even his own life, he cannot be my disciple.* (ESV)

These verses, especially the one from Luke, are shocking to me. How could I hate this little guy?

Certainly, I'm not to hate my children, parents or siblings, but God is showing me another aspect of his love. The love of God for us, and our responsive love to him, should make even the deepest family love look like hate in comparison.

God's love is so enormous it makes the love we have even for our own children look like hate.

First John 3:1 tells us of the quality of his love: *See how very much our heavenly Father loves us, for he allows us to be called his children and we really are!* (NLT)

This is the manner or quality of his love. God understands an earthly father's love for his children. He calls us His children.

It has now been almost thirty-one years since I held Jonathan David Buck on that early Valentine's Day morning.

He grew up, wrestled with God, but eventually made his faith his own. He married his high school sweetheart, went to seminary and is now a pastor. He and his wife have dedicated their lives to building a Godly heritage.

Three years ago, they had their first child, a baby boy. They named him Jonathan David Buck Jr.

When I held him in my arms, my first grandchild, I experienced another aspect of love, stretching my heart even more. I knew that God had answered Betsy's and my prayers and desires. A new Godly heritage had begun.

I no longer try to fit my comprehension of God's love in my mind. God is love. I believe now that the quality of God's love was never meant to fit in our minds, only in our hearts.

~ Rob Buck

A baby is God's opinion that the world should go on.

Carl Sandburg

18
From One Stage to Another

By the time my first child learned to articulate, another was trying her wings at vocabulary. And after a while translating that childish language was like learning a new one.

Stage 1: Learning the Vernacular — Translation

1.	Toothpick with hair	Q-tip
2.	Muscle sprouts	brussel sprouts
3.	Rubber band and on ice cream	bandaid on first-aid cream
4.	Firtfleen	thirteen
5.	Macabloney	macaroni
6.	Blockley	broccoli
7.	Undershoulders	underarms
8.	Cantaloupe	kaleidoscope
9.	Magic Flying Glass	magnifying glass
10.	Donald Duck's	McDonald's
11.	She is "agabakin" me!	aggravating
12.	Pooky tories	spooky stories
13.	Anpipple	pineapple

I no longer even wince when one of the younger ones explains that she soaked her foot in "turkey-time" (turpentine) to get the black tar off it.

When four-year-old David was asked to be a crown bearer at a Valentine's Day Banquet, we were not at all concerned about whether he knew himself to be an animal, vegetable or mineral as, all decked out in a new black suit, bow tie and red carnation boutonniere he exclaimed, "Boy I can't wait 'til I'm a cranberry!"

Stage 2: Learning to Spell

After David started to school, he asked, "Mommy, how do you spell tomato?"
"T-o-m-a-t-o."

"Oh," he said, " All you have to do is take that "T" off, put a "B" and you've got Buhtato."

Cindy, then three, became fascinated with the reading process. We took turns listening. One of her reading books had an adorable picture of a jar with a bee on it, with the word "H-O-N-E-Y" underneath. Try as we might, we were unable to convince her that the word was not "Bee-jelly."

Stage 3: Questioning

"Does your head get empty if your hair all comes out?
"Mommy, where's the dark?"
"How do you get up to heaven when you die?"

Lisa rushed in from school very excited. "You know what?" she said. "A girl in my class fell over her puppy and broke her elbow." Cindy asked placidly, "*What's* her *name?*"

I had been chatting with a friend and didn't want to use the woman's name, nor come out and say the woman was a liar. So, trying to be kind, I said, "That woman from Mississippi seems to fantasize a lot." Cindy looked up from her coloring and asked, "What about Mrs. Hippie's panty size?"

A mother learns to be careful in analyzing the meaning and in answering questions. You learn not to say, "Absolutely not! One's enough for anybody!" and you even understand they're only referring to a certain brand of sucker when they ask, "Can I have another dumb pop?"

Stage 4: Answers for Everything

When he was three, David related, "One time I was swimming in the water and a shark bit off my legs."

I pointed to his legs. "What do you call those things?"

With a lift of his chin, he answered without a blink of his eyelashes, "They grew back."

Another time, he was standing quite still in his room. Finally I commented, "David. It looks like your pants are getting wet."

He shook his head, indicating I was mistaken.

"Well," I said. "Just what is happening?"

In a calm voice, he replied, "My pants are sweating."

Howard took David to the grocery store with him and the check-out lady said, "We're giving away free Cokes today. Do you want them?"

"Certainly," Howard replied. "Thank you."

David — unable to talk plainly, but able to count up to ten — looked wide-eyed at the woman when she put a couple of Cokes in the bag, then at his dad and asserted loudly, "That's not 'free' Cokes. That's only two."

When David was debating his sisters about Santa Claus, the Easter Bunny, and the Tooth Fairy, he said there was no tooth fairy. His sisters, old enough to know they had to believe if they were to get their quarters, asserted, "There certainly is."

"Is not," he said. "That's just Mom dressed up like one."

~ *Yvonne Lehman*

19

The Guatemala Mission

I waved goodbye to my family and friends on a cold January morning in 2013, anticipating the mission that lay ahead. The mixture of adrenaline and thankfulness to be on another mission trip to Guatemala warmed my spirit and calmed pre-flight jitters as our team drove to the airport.

It was hard to believe how time had flown by since July 2011. God had moved in amazing ways on that trip. The children at the malnutrition center touched our lives and changed us, forever. I couldn't wait to hug all those precious children again.

A family friend, Howie Hooper, had been working with Orphan's Heart as a team leader and director for a few years. He's led countless mission teams in Haiti, Guatemala, Honduras, Africa, and the Dominican Republic. He asked me if I'd be willing to share our team's experiences and be the mission blogger for our week in Guatemala.

"Yes!" I said without hesitation. "I'd love to."

"Thanks Joann, I'm thrilled and grateful to spend time with your church's Go Team. I'm sure we're all going to have an amazing week ahead of us."

I smiled at the thought that Howie and our Go Team Missions Pastor, Jonathan (J.P.) Pearson, were a perfect pair of leaders for our group. I only wished my husband, Dennis, could have come too. Before we left, Dennis told me, "Maybe I can go another time. But I can't leave work now. I want you to go. Do what God called you to do — and remember, I love you. Have a great time."

So we prayed together and asked God to fulfill His will for the team in Guatemala. I ended our prayer time with, "Thank you, Lord, for answering prayers for this team to go into the world as your hands and feet. Amen."

When the flight landed, my first sights and sounds included the majestic mountains, gigantic volcanoes, modern buildings, busy traffic, and smells of diesel in Guatemala City. We had our first meal at a typical fast food restaurant, Pollo Campero. Then we drove west. The cooler air flowed through the windows in the cramped, rickety bus, as we climbed away from the city. Finally Antigua's cobblestone roads, fresher air, and the majestic Agua volcano welcomed us with open arms.

After we settled in at the hotel, our team planned our adventures for Sunday. In our rooms we listened to the sounds of the city. Fireworks and music sounded long into the night. But that's not what kept me awake. I could barely sleep because I knew God had an amazing week planned for us.

I woke up to the sounds of birds singing. During breakfast, Howie said, "For more than one hyndred years the Florida Baptist Children's Homes has been working to serve abused, neglected and orphaned children in Florida and now we are also reaching out to serve children in the developing world. Together we can be witnesses of the love of Jesus Christ to the least of these, in Florida and to the ends of the earth."

And so our mission officially began.

On the first day, we explored the area. We left the hotel in a huge jeep-like vehicle with seats in the back that only had a ladder access. After a scary ride up the steep mountain on rough roads, some of the group toured a coffee plantation, others zip-lined.

I wanted to savor every moment of that beautiful morning in Antigua. Soon my favorite word of day was "awesome." I went with the adventurous, or crazy, group that did the two long one-quarter to one-half mile zips across the breathtaking canyon. We flew five hundred feet above the tree line. We spent the rest of the day enjoying the sights, the people, and feeling that God was smiling with us. Later that night I wrote my first blog post.

> Today is awesome because God is getting us ready for the week ahead. We faced our fears of the unknown together, and grew stronger. We became a team. Now we can take on and savor all the upcoming adventures and challenges tomorrow has for us. I can't wait! Because tomorrow is about the children.

The long awaited day dawned. We set out early in the morning for the Malnutrition Center. The hour-long ride gave us valuable information about Guatemala's agriculture and cultural diversities and traditions. We were greeted with dozens of beautiful smiling faces. My heart melted when I saw all those familiar faces I had fallen in love with a year and a half before. The team played, sang, and changed tons of diapers. We blew bubbles and gave lots of hugs. We saw how God's grace can heal and change lives when a young mother came with her pastor.

I read my second post out loud before I pressed send.

> This is a special place. The Center's staff and the interpreters, Alejandra and Olivia, were angels-in-disguise. We came here hoping to be God's hands and feet. But the children are his heart. I'm so thankful to be here. This is another day I will remember for the rest of my life, and it is only day three.

I witnessed God's love in action over the next several days. The children at the Malnutrition Center were all strikingly beautiful. All had their own special quality that set them apart from the others. We bonded with them. I gave many haircuts. They loved it. So did I. Our team continued to testify about all our wow-moments, like the ways the children responded to our touch, our voices, our hugs and kisses, or the way they showed their unconditional love and concern for each other. They are a family brought together by God. Sure they loved singing, playing outside, puzzle and puppet time. I sensed they craved being held and hugged. And yes, there was laughter and some tears. But it was the quiet moments that penetrated our hearts and broke through the language and cultural barriers. The prayers. The power. The serenity of God's presence was undeniably felt by all. And so I wrote:

> He is their strength, their hope, their bread and breath. The light and life of all the world. I can't wait till tomorrow.

Throughout the week, our team enjoyed many more wow-moments. We felt God's presence and watched Him move in mighty ways as we worked at the center. A few ladies worked with the infants (Canaries) all week. On the last ride back to the hotel, my friend Nancy said, "I've been loving on this sweet little girl since Monday, and today she finally smiled at me."

A few of the other ladies shared similar stories. Wanda spent time with the center's doctor discussing several infants' progress. "I'm thankful for these sweet moments we all shared today," she said. "I'm also thankful for my friends who have taken tons of pictures this week. And for everyone loving the children (Chicks, Bunnies, Squirrels, and Ducks) like they were their own."

The center workers thanked us for all the repairs our team made inside and around the property while the children took their naps. After the treacherous ride back to Antigua, my roommate, Gloria, said, "I'm thankful for Samuel's driving skills…really!"

Everyone clapped.

That night I wrote:

> I'm thankful for how great you are, Lord. Today my favorite word is "thankful." Please help me. I'm finding it hard to leave this place.

The sun shone bright the next morning. It was time to say goodbye. Once again we stepped out in faith. We said our goodbyes to the children we had grown to love, believing, we would be back.

While on the plane back to the states, I wrote:

> The wow-moments were far too many to list, but I know every moment soaked into our souls. I pray the memories of this week never slip away. Each child gave us a wow-moment. Some made us cry, some made us laugh. Some made us hold our noses! Each touched our lives in a very real and powerful way. We will miss them all, so much.

As the end of our journey drew near I longed to see my family. I thought about the last words my husband had said to me when I left. "Remember I love you." His words filled my heart as if he were sharing a word from God who loves us no matter where we live or what we do. He wants to go with us.

I believe we're all called to go out into the world. That may be in our own neighborhood, city, state, or another country. The location doesn't matter. What matters is that we share the love of the Father and his son, Jesus. And we allow our lives to be touched, and filled by others, especially children.

I'm thankful to have had the chance to be part of the Orphan's Heart team. They are a group of ordinary people living the extraordinary message Jesus preached. I'll treasure every precious moment.

- Joann M. Claypoole

20

God Rocks

We had been hiking for only forty-five minutes, but being the indoor sort of person I am, I was on the verge of being miserable. I wasn't used to such physical torture and was not enjoying it in the least. I was a secretary accustomed to sitting at my desk in an air-conditioned office, exerting no more physical energy than it took to click my mouse or run a photocopy or scribble something in my day planner.

When my little girl asked me to go on a hiking trip through the jungle with her and her outdoorsy uncle, I knew I wouldn't enjoy it much, but I also could not look into those pleading hazel-blue eyes on that Sunday afternoon and find a reasonable excuse to refuse her. So, the three of us put on our grungy clothes, our thickest-soled, no-snake-can-bite-through-these shoes, filled our water bottles, piled into my Corolla, and headed to the State Park for Cissy's first-ever hiking adventure.

Considering the fact that we were moving slowly to allow Cissy's five-year-old legs to keep pace with us over the muddy, rocky hiking trail, we were making pretty good time. Cissy was absolutely enthralled by all of the new things she was seeing in the big forest, which was really not much more than a small slice of Ohio woodlands. But when one is five years old, the smallest trees look massive, the smallest spiders look monstrous, and the smallest animal noises sound mysterious and intriguing.

To be perfectly honest, though, I was far from being intrigued. I didn't verbalize my complaints because I didn't want to spoil the experience for my little Jungle Jane, but it was very obvious to my brother that I was longing for my air-conditioned house, my remote control, and my comfortable Sunday afternoon napping sofa.

By the time we reached the bridge that crossed the widest part of the river I was hot, tired, and ready to find my way back to the indoors for a shower and a fresh pair of dry socks. I was bug-bitten, sweaty from head to toe, and could have sworn that poison ivy was setting in at that very moment.

Frankly, I was ready to turn back. I trekked on behind my brother and my daughter, wishing every minute that I'd hear her beg, "Mommy, I'm tired. Can we go home now?" but she never complained — not once. For the first time in my life, I was actually longing to hear those inevitable childish words, "Are we there yet?" but she said nothing of the sort. So, on we trudged.

It wasn't until some time later that I realized the beauty of what was going on inside that brain and heart of hers as we trudged on through the hot, muggy Midwestern Ohio foliage. We walked up the riverbank a bit to a shady area completely surrounded by cliffs and rocks and boulders. It reminded me of something out of an old Western movie except for the manmade bridges, No Trespassing — Flora Preserve Area signs in certain areas of the terrain, and the park rangers riding by occasionally on mountain bikes.

As we walked up a slight incline, which caused me to huff and puff a bit and wish all the more that I was at home, my daughter sighed in awe. "Mommy, God rocks!" she exclaimed.

At first, I wasn't sure what she meant. When she went on to explain, I was completely impressed by her perceptiveness and utterly ashamed of my own nonchalant ungratefulness.

"God rocks, Mom! Over there," she repeated, pointing toward two huge boulders larger than my family room. "See them, Uncle Jay?" She motioned for my brother to witness the wonder.

"What do you mean?" I asked.

She sighed, put her hands on her hips and rolled her eyes, obviously upset with me for not sharing in her excitement. "They're God rocks, 'cause if God wasn't holding them up like that, they'd fall right off the edge."

Gazing at them again, I realized she was absolutely right! The boulders were sitting precariously, with what appeared to be the greater portion of their huge mass hanging over the edge of the cliff. There seemed to be no plausible reason they should not tumble down into the river below.

Those were God rocks indeed, and in the midst of my unimpressed, complaining spirit, I had forgotten that every leaf we had brushed past, every crawdad we'd seen scurring out from under the rocks on the riverbank, and every cricket we'd heard were divinely created for a reason. Maybe that reason was just for our pleasure and enjoyment. Maybe that reason was to reveal to Cissy — and to once again remind me — how big and strong God is and how much he rocks.

My daughter accepted Christ in March of 2003. There is no greater joy than seeing how God reveals himself to her little by little, day by day. The scriptures tell us that creation is a testimony of God's power and divinity. Those God rocks revealed that to us in a visible language simple enough for a five-year-old and her indifferent mother to understand. Romans 1:18 (NIV) tells us, *since the creation of the world, God's invisible qualities — His eternal power and divine nature — have been clearly seen, being understood from what has been made, so that men are without excuse.*

Whether we are desk jockeys or nature lovers, it is important to remember that when we compare his greatness to our own fatigue or scientific logic or even the beauty of nature, we will find it very true indeed that God rocks!

- Autumn Conley

21
Name Them One by One

I consider myself a thankful person. I thank God before every meal and truly appreciate all that has been given me. Well, at least I thought I did, until my four-year-old son redefined how thankful I was.

It was bedtime, and like me and my siblings when we were young, my son has been known to try and delay the inevitable…sleep. This particular night he decided he wanted to pray. I closed my eyes but then peeked at him, and saw him sitting up with eyes wide open, but saying, "Thank you God for my house, the sea, the mountains, the grass, my clothes…"

He began to look around the room as I wondered how long this would go on. He obviously wasn't aware that nighttime is the only alone time my husband and I have together.

"…and thank you for the lamps, the paint on the walls, the bed, the light bulbs…"

I hate to admit it but I found myself starting to get frustrated. Was he doing this just so he wouldn't have to lie down? He's smart enough to know that I won't interrupt while he is praying.

"….and thank you for my stuffed animals, my friends, my mommy and daddy, and that I won't have any bad dreams tonight. Amen."

He smiled and lay down. That's when I realized he truly was thankful and I should have more gratitude in my life. After all, what would my life be like without a bed, walls around me, lamps, clothes, food? The list could go on and on. God gives us so many gifts that we take them for granted. We should be thankful for every thing, no matter how big or small they seem.

That night I thanked God for our little boy, as always, but I was even more thankful that through my son's heartfelt prayer of naming out loud the many things for which he was thankful, I was reminded of how many good gifts I've been given.

I became more aware that my prayers shouldn't simply be, "Thank you for my blessings." Instead of lumping them all together it's a good idea not to take the seemingly small things for granted, but name them as the words of a song tells us, "Count your many blessings. Name them one by one."

- Cindy Wilson

22
Tripping Over Alligators

While on vacation my family and I rode past by a little country church, tucked away in the hollows of North Carolina's Smoky Mountains. We decided to make that our destination for worship the next morning.

As my wife, our two daughters ages five and two, and I piled out of the car, my thoughts centered around the smallness of the church, the isolated location. My mind envisioned snake-handling possibilities.

The parking lot was gravel, and its underbelly displayed red clay which had oozed up to the surface from the last time it rained. A handful of cars lined one side, and there were no lines to inform us where to park. Just a vague, rough line of where the gravel ended and the grass began.

We strolled up to the front door, and I opened it. We were immediately in the sanctuary. There was no vestibule. No foyer. No hallway. No welcoming deacon. Just center stage. The proverbial spotlight shone brightly on us as several heads turned.

Pre-worship music played in the background, lilting softly across the rectangular room, the congregation's cue to stop talking about last night's fried chicken dinner, and instead, get their minds right with the Holy Spirit.

So, we slinked inside, slid stage right, and sat on the very hard back pew. A robust woman, in a fashionable dress from the late-1960s (if I recalled correctly), tickled the ivories much like a piano man at a bar in some TV sitcom, but with more stilted reverence one would find in an Episcopalian church.

Then, in a motion akin to a movie star approaching the podium at the Academy Awards, the pastor stood from his wing-backed chair on the platform and sprang over to the pulpit.

"Please stand," he said in a pleasant voice, "and turn to page such-n-such, and let's sing a hymn." I don't recollect the hymn or the page number. But we stood. And we sang…and we sang…and we sang…all the hymns listed on the board with the little metal mailbox numbers. Five hymns, I seem to recall. Or maybe it was three. But yes, we sang…all the verses.

After the congregational singing, a special hymn was performed by a lady who sang beautifully loud during the other hymns. She belted out the hymn with the flare one can only appreciate if one were there.

And yes. She sang all the verses.

Finally, we sat down, and the pastor began to speak.

At first, he started in a slow, conversational, polite manner. We opened our Bibles and read the selected scripture of the day. New Testament. Book of Matthew, if memory serves. Red letters, for sure.

All seemed normal enough, whatever that looks like.

However, as the pastor got wound up, the almost disc jockey tone of this stout gentleman devolved into a low growl. The low growl became augmented by purposeful, regimented stresses on certain words. It was diction with a purpose. Especially when he used the phrase, "Jesus said."

"Jesus said, 'The just shall live by faith.'"

"And Jesus said, 'If the Son has set you free, you are free indeed.'"

"And Jesus said…"

You get the idea.

As he continued to heat up, the ever-increasing growl morphed into a snarling, spitting, snorting exposition of God's Word. The words got louder. The talk got faster. The sweat rolled down his face. And it was then when the pastor burst into full hell fire and brimstone glory, complete with a handkerchief and an occasional wipe of his mouth and forehead.

Our oldest daughter leaned over to my wife, and in the innocence only a five-year-old girl could convey, said, "Mommy, why is that man shouting?"

Now, as you know, the words from a child often do not come with a volume switch. So my wife, trying not to draw any more attention to our already established limelight, leaned down and mouthed a quiet "Shhh" before saying, "That's just the way he preaches, honey."

To which my daughter replied in more than a whisper, "He sounds like he has an alligator biting his leg."

What do you do with that?

Do you know how hard it was to keep a straight face? Every time the pastor snarled the words, "Jesus said," my fiction writer's fertile mind pictured a large reptile gripping his leg, spinning him in a death roll. It was apparent my wife was watching the same movie-of-the-mind. Her blood-red face was proof positive.

I have to admit, we really don't remember anything the pastor said after that moment…except the phrase, "Jesus said."

I do remember the handkerchief, though, for I'd never seen a preacher froth at the mouth before.

It was…interesting. And a little disturbing.

After we left the church, I found myself reflecting. *How could God use that? That whole scene? That entire sermon? That display of what seemed to be more showmanship than God-centered worship and biblical exposition. No wonder they had only ten people in that church. And those hard, wooden pews… come on…get into the 21st century…will ya?*

Skewed by the church growth movement of the day, as we drove away I questioned everything about these believers and their church, right down to the clapboard siding and gravel parking lot. It was definitely a lesson in how not to grow a church.

Over the years, I have thought many times about that lazy Sunday morning. Now I've become older and, hopefully, a smidgen wiser.

The Apostle Paul, wrote to the Church in Philippi while he sat in a prison cell: *It is true that some preach Christ out of envy and rivalry, but others out of goodwill. The latter do so out of love, knowing that I am put here for the defense of the gospel. The former preach Christ out of selfish ambition, not sincerely, supposing that they can stir up trouble for me while I am in chains. But what does it matter? The important thing is that in every way, whether from false motives or true, Christ is preached. And because of this I rejoice.* (Philippians 1:15-18 NIV)

Did you catch that? Paul said that so long as Christ is preached then he didn't really care what mode was used or what the motives of the messenger were. Preaching about Christ was the key.

Why? Because when Christ is preached, God can still move and work and woo sinners to himself. God can use anyone to expand his kingdom.

Had I been more in tune with the Holy Spirit instead of the spirit of the church growth movement, I would have found my daughter's comment funny, but not in the same way.

Was the pastor's method of preaching weird? To us, yes. But to the regular attenders? No. They were receptive. They responded appropriately. "Amens" and "Hallelujahs" shot out like blasts from a duck hunter behind a blind. Short. Loud. Timely. Heart-felt.

When we trip over alligators, it causes us to miss the gospel message. When we trust in our book learning and think we're enlightened beyond the scope of Christ-centered salvation, it must sadden our Heavenly Father.

While I tried to contain myself from laughing at crucial and critical, decision-making moments in that pastor's sermon, I fell prey to the temptation of tripping over alligators.

The naiveté of a child proved to be the fire used to burn the dross and refine the metal of one of God's older children, showing me the error of my judgmental ways.

For as it is written in Isaiah 11:6, *a little child will lead them.*

~ C. Kevin Thompson

23
Rich in Love

When my twin boys were young, we struggled financially to keep it together. Their father had chosen not to live with us and I was forced to find a way to provide a home for my children on my own. Being young myself, I did not know all the recommended ways to rear children, and all the ways to be the perfect mom. At the time, we were living hours away from my family and had no help or support from them. All I had to go on was what I remembered from my own childhood, and the way I remembered my grandmother had reared my sister and me.

I was always honest with the boys and told them just what our situation was, and why I could not buy the same things for them the other kids at school had. They knew what we had God had provided for us, and that was enough. We had what was necessary, enjoyed that fact and were thankful.

I always made sure they knew I loved them, and that they should love each other. They got a hug and kiss each night when I put them to bed and I made a point of saying, "I love you" to them at every opportunity.

When they were in second grade, Bobby's teacher assigned the class to write a paragraph. I knew nothing about it, and when he brought home the paper, the teacher had written a very kind note on it. Of course, I was pleased that he had received such a good mark and the praise of his teacher, but when I read his little essay, I wept. I still do, just thinking about it, even after all these years. Apparently, something I had been trying to teach them had sunk in more than I realized.

In his childish scrawl, he had written a few words about his home and family. And the most memorable line he wrote was, "We don't have lots of money, but we are rich of love."

How often I had told them that we did not have to have money to be rich, I do not remember, but I had said it every time they wanted to know why they could not have whatever new brand name item their friends had. My grandmother had often told us that we were rich in love though we did not have the same advantages as our friends. I wanted my sons to know that love would make them rich as nothing else could do. Even at their tender age, they understood this.

Today, we each have more material things than we did then, but more important, we still love each other. Love is the one thing that we will never lose, and love can never be taken away from us.

~ Virginia Foreman

24
The "Think" Blessing

Praying aloud in public is a problem for me, and I attribute it to memorized prayers. Therefore, I decided to teach my children to make up their own prayers.

The first comment was, "I can't thank God for worms. They don't taste good."

The first *homemade* prayer came out, "Thank you God for frogs."

It was terribly difficult to keep my composure. I lectured myself on the value of frogs, trying to picture them as cute sitting on a lily-pad, but for the life of me I could only visualize a deep-throated "crruuump" from a warty, scaly, bulgy-eyed, long-tongued fly catcher.

By trial and error I learned to guide my children in their prayers, like, "When we're eating vegetables it would be nice to thank God for vegetables and save the frog and worm prayer until you're outside…etc."

Lori, the oldest, understood and no problem was presented by my second child, Lisa, who always copied Lori.

As the years passed and we added David and Cindy, other problems arose. The baby, Cindy, always chimed in with squeals of delight at having folded her hands, which often drove the other three into hysterics. Finally it simmered down to applause (a little enthusiasm before meals isn't too bad!) and eventually graduated into hand folding and mumbling.

They soon became so enthusiastic it became a daily fight about who was going to say the blessing. They would rush to the table screaming, "first-first!" and the first to scream was "it."

In our family no one wants to be second. So it often ended in hurt feelings (usually in my hands) accusations of "she was first last," pouting, being sent to bedrooms, then eventually a half-hearted duty-blessing.

So, we developed a plan whereby each child was scheduled the same day each week. I carefully explained that when one says the blessing, the others can be second, third, etc. if they wish, or the others can "think" a blessing.

They seemed to go for the idea of thinking a blessing. I explained that God knows what we mean when we think it. We do not always have to pray aloud.

I was amazed at the response to the "think" blessing. With one blessing rather than six (my husband and I had our turns too), we were able to eat hot meals again.

One night, after putting the children to bed for the last time and turning out the light, I returned to the living room for my nightly deep sigh of relief.

After a few moments the silence was interrupted by the patter of little feet and Lisa stood before me, very calm and self-satisfied.

"What are you doing up?" I asked sternly.

She answered in all seriousness, "I can stay up. I thinked it."

Sometimes I'm a little slow so I asked the inevitable. "You thinked what?"

"I thinked going to sleep, and God knows what I mean, so now I can stay up."

…atleastitsneverdull…

~ Yvonne Lehman

Always be nice to your children
because they are the ones who will choose your rest home.

Phyllis Diller

25
Don't Be an Artist

I was pregnant with our first child. Todd and I were on our way home from my final OBGYN appointment. Everything looked great. We were just waiting for the little one — the first grandchild of our parents — to make her appearance.

I turned to Todd in complete sincerity and stammered, "What if the baby wants to be an artist?"

He didn't understand the question.

"You know, if she's artsy, like an actor or musician or painter, what are we going to do then?"

He blinked.

Trying again, I said, "I won't know how to handle someone whose success hinges on whether or not people get them. Seems like it's not a real job, you know? I mean, being a grown up means having some kind of measurable success, right?"

Todd shrugged. Probably the safest way to end that hormone-driven conversation, as well as evidence that he did not share my concern.

Unquantifiable artistic talent was my biggest fear. Not illness or accident. Not being gay. Not atheism. Not tattoos or purple hair. Not an unplanned pregnancy. I know that my faith and family can weather all those things. I most feared her being misunderstood or not celebrated for her uniqueness.

She wasn't even born yet and I was worried about her being a grown up.

But first, she'd need to go to school. I went to junior high and high school with a girl who became an opera singer. Several former classmates have done serious work in clothing design and music and...art.

I remember these people and their uniqueness when they were young.

After the birth and growth of my daughter, accompanied by more reasonable hormones, I thought about the arts. They inspire. They are memorable. They can be blended beautifully with our everyday careers to make something ordinary something extraordinary.

Amazing things happen when God-given talent and hard work join. So now, many years later, I don't want my daughter to be an artist; I want her to use the gifts God has given her, reach her potential, and use her creativity in a career that challenges and inspires her and others.

But wouldn't it be just precious if she became an artist!

~ Christina Krost

26

Barren but Filled

My mind had raced all day. I just wanted to make it home. I'd promised myself I wouldn't take a test until my monthly period was at least a week late. Today was day six. But one day really didn't make that much of a difference and I couldn't stand it any longer. Just what if I was finally carrying our baby? Just what if?

My husband and I were two years into what seemed like a very long winter season of our souls.

As I reached into the back of the cabinet that held a stockpile of pregnancy tests, I wondered if this was it. Was this the one? Would I take pictures of this stick? Would I leave it on the counter for my husband or scream at him when he walked in the door? This one stick could change our lives and take away my barren label forever.

But this test could also pierce to the deepest part of my heart. Would days pass before I would feel so-called-normal again? Would this test brand me, again? Barren. Empty. Broken.

As I waited the three minutes like I had done a thousand times before, my heart bounced back and forth from despair to excitement. I prayed as I waited, "God, help me believe you are good if this test says No."

Then…one…very lonely…pink line appeared.

I shoved the stick under the trash. How foolish was I to think the test could possibly be positive? After all this time, I should have known better. Was God good? Really good? My head knew the right answer, but I couldn't make my heart believe.

I remembered nights I'd walked the floor, pouring my wounded and very weary heart out before God. There was actually a spot in our old house next to my side of the bed where the carpet was worn. And the Lord was right there. At times, I could feel his strong, scarred hands wrap around my broken heart.

At times I would scream, so angry at him for making me walk this road. Ugly, so ugly, I knew. But he was there then too. He listened. And softly whispered back, "I will never stop loving you. You cannot push me away. I will always chase after you."

I was silent too. Mostly because there weren't words to describe my pain. But God knew the pain. His Spirit groaned for me when I didn't have the words. My ache for a child hurt so badly. The longing to be a mother was great. After all, he placed that desire in my heart when I was just a little girl. All I wanted to do was to grow up and be a mommy.

After another journey — our adoption journey — springtime came for our hearts. We brought Selah Grace home. God wrote his faithfulness all over her sweet story. She brought healing to my heart.

There is a frequent misconception that after adoption, because one is a mother, the barrenness subsides, that it magically disappears. Although the ache to be a mother has been filled, my barren womb is just that, still barren.

It is hard work sorting through the feelings, and grieving the kicks I never felt from Selah. Hot tears burn my face because I never saw her movement in my womb from an ultrasound. When these feelings surface, instead of fighting and pushing the Lord away, I let him bring my heart to a place of acceptance.

I lean in close to him when my best friend tells me of her pregnancy. I nestle up close to his heart, when I ache that I never had the chance to carry the child living in my home. I run to his lap at the reminder of my barrenness at the end of every month. And it hurts. Still. So much.

But the nearness of him, the intimacy that he and I now share over this barren womb of mine, is something I would never trade for a thousand yes-sticks.

And when I'm driving and my precious girl babbles away in her car seat, singing to worship music, I thank God for my barren womb, because he gave me sweet grace, my sweet Selah Grace.

~ *Jessica Satterfield*

27
Backwards Party in a Hoghouse

In my earliest memory of writing my own thoughts and ideas I recall playing with secret codes. My older brother, Keith, had been exchanging messages in code with Ronnie who lived on the farm up the road. I was in the second grade and thought it looked like fun.

The easiest code they were writing called for two sheets of paper and a piece of carbon paper. The trick was getting the papers in the right position before starting to write — an original copy on top, a second sheet under that which would carry the encoded message, and beneath it all was a sheet of carbon paper with the carbon side up. Then when you wrote the message correctly on the top sheet of paper, it would appear backwards on the backside of the second sheet of paper. It was a great trick!

I realized two problems with my newfound trick, though. The first was figuring out who to write a message to since my older brother preferred writing to the neighbor boy, and my younger brothers and sister couldn't yet read. The second problem was figuring out what to say in my secret message if I wrote one. This was probably my first encounter with writer's block.

That's when the idea of writing an invitation to a party came to me. Since the writing was all backwards, it seemed perfect for an invitation to a backwards party.

The Sunday school department at our church had recently held a backwards party where everyone dressed with their clothes on backwards or wrong side out, and with their shoes on the wrong feet.

My family had recently moved to the family farm in Rochester, Indiana, which had been issued as a grant from the Northwest Territory to one of our ancestors. There was also a new family who had moved into the farmhouse across the road, and they had four young children. I could invite them to join us for a backwards party in our clubhouse.

With Mama's permission, I wrote the invitation, in code of course, and took it to Mrs. Deloris Ogle across the road. She didn't understand it, so I showed her how to hold it up to a mirror to read it. And what joy! She said they would come to my party!

When the day arrived for the party, the girls, Carol and Doris, came in dresses though I don't recall what her son, Donnie, wore. They didn't wear anything wrong side out or backwards.

I panicked! I guess in all the excitement I had forgotten to explain to Mrs. Ogle about our clubhouse.

The clubhouse was nothing more than an abandoned five by seven foot hog-house behind the barn. To fix it up for the party we had brushed out the spider webs and used some crepe paper to attempt to make it more festive. I had also planned an activity or two to play in it. But I would *never* wear one of my dresses to play in the clubhouse. We even had to climb in through the door in the roof.

If it bothered Mrs. Ogle, she never let on. She let the children take their clothes off and put them back on wrong side out and backwards. And the party began! I was quite proud to have pulled off the party, but I also learned something about the importance of including all the important details in an invitation.

~ Janice D. Green

28
Bowling, Fishing, and Dancing

BUMPER BOWLING

I watched as my granddaughter, Katelyn, rolled the pink bowling ball in the carousel until her five-year-old fingers found the holes to slide into. She picked up the six-pound ball and in a wobbly run made her way to the foul line where she came to an abrupt stop.

Swinging her small upper body to the right, she brought the ball up with both hands and heaved it down the bowling lane. Thump. Thump. Thump. The ball dribbled out of control, and then made contact with the lane where it swirled from the right gutter to the left gutter and once more to the right. Slowly, it reached the pins and knocked over all ten.

With a celebratory jump, Katelyn smiled. "Yes! a strike."

Katelyn was Bumper Bowling, a game for children, which meant her ball was protected from falling into the gutters by pads positioned on each side of the bowling lane.

Marital problems, health issues and financial concerns had left me feeling like a bowling ball dropped and thumped from one crisis to the next before swirling out of control, rolling into the gutter and landing in a pit. Faced with so many difficult decisions, I didn't know what to pray for, so I prayed as David did in Psalm 25, *"Show me your ways, O Lord, teach me your paths."* If I could get out of the pit and onto the Lord's path, I would find the hope and peace promised in God's Word.

Remembering Katelyn's Bumper Bowling, I asked the Lord to place bumpers so I couldn't veer from his path. "Lord," I prayed, "I want to go Bumper Bowling."

Reading God's Word, talking with him in prayer, and seeking wise counsel are bumpers that can keep us from veering off his path and landing in the pit.

Goin' Fishing

"I'm going fishin', Nana," my three-year-old granddaughter said.

I smiled to myself as KK walked out of the kitchen where I stood washing dishes. *How cute.* I imagined KK casting out an imaginary fishing line and reeling in her plastic fish.

Suddenly my smile vanished as I recalled some of KK's previous escapades. With sudsy water dripping from my hands, I dashed down the hall to the bathroom, all the while envisioning the tub overflowing with water and plastic fish.

Instead, I saw KK slowly emerging into the hallway — from the den. As she walked toward me, she cautiously placed one small foot down and then the other. In one hand she held a paper cup while her other hand covered the top of the cup. Upon reaching me, KK removed her hand from the cup and said, "Look Nana, I caught a fish."

Peering into the cup of sloshing water, I recognized a fish that had been kidnapped, or fishnapped, from its home in the aquarium.

KK was serious about her fishing. She never intended to use a make-believe fishing pole to catch plastic fish. KK was determined to catch real fish.

Simon and Andrew were fishermen casting their nets into the lake when Jesus came along. They were serious about their fishing, using nets and catching "real fish." Yet Jesus told them that he had a more important fishing assignment for them — to be fishers of men.

Even today, Jesus calls us to do the same. Do we hear his voice saying, "Come, and follow me"? Are we willing to leave behind our busyness as Simon and Andrew did? Are we willing to share the good news of Jesus Christ with a lost and hurting world? Are we willing to be *serious* fishers of men?

Snow Dance

His bald head glowed, his brown eyes sparkled, and his toothless grin made my heart skip a beat. His right arm rested on my shoulder while his left hand grasped mine as we twirled around in the kitchen. Cole laughed. For now, anyway, he seemed to think dancing with Nana was fun.

I looked into the eyes of this five-month-old grandson of mine and relished the pure innocence of his life, as yet, untouched by the world.

"When God looks down at you, Baby Cole," I said, "He sees you as white as snow."

We twirled again. "And when God looks down at me—" Suddenly the trance was broken.

My life has been touched by the world, and I have sinned greatly.

Satan, the great deceiver and peace-stealer, used this opportunity to hiss past sins at me. I could imagine the ugly, jagged scars on my soul. Our twirling slowed, and came to a stop as I felt my heart sink. Baby Cole's smile faded, and he looked at me as if to ask, "Why did we stop dancing? What happened to our joy?"

The Lord spoke to my heart and reminded me of truth.

I know who I am. I am a child of the King. God loves me so much that he sent his one and only Son, Jesus, into the world. Jesus paid the price for me, Baby Cole, and all of mankind when he shed his blood on the cross. All I have to do was believe in him, and not only does he forgive my sins, I have the promise of eternal life with him in heaven.

My sins have been forgiven.

My sins have even been forgotten.

My sins have been removed from me as far as the east is from the west.

I looked back into Cole's eyes, and the magical moment returned.

~ Susan Dollyhigh

29
The Hollows of Our Hearts

I had a feeling of déjà vu the morning my son Ted called to say he was taking his pregnant wife to the hospital because of contractions. "No problem," he said. "Just a precaution." Deb's due date was five weeks away. An hour later he called back to invite me to the birthing room since Deb's mother was out of town. All systems were "Go."

As my husband and I drove through morning rain, I was fearful. Twenty years earlier, at the same time of year, five weeks before my due date, I had given birth to our only daughter.

But early on that first day of April, our cries shattered the dawn, not hers. Doctors couldn't explain Christy's under-developed lungs, and a few hours later she found heaven's air easier to breath. I felt God had played a cruel April Fool's Day joke on us. Now I wondered if one tragedy was not enough for our family.

When we met Ted and Deb in the birthing room Angie the nurse was upbeat. "Everything's perfect," she insisted. The baby's heart pounded a soft drumbeat through a monitor. I held Deb's hand as Ted went for breakfast.

When Ted returned, they discussed names — David William, William David — playing with grandfathers' names in case Deb gave birth to a boy. Holly, Jacqueline, Allison, Elizabeth. They asked my opinion of girls' names, and I reminded them they had previously considered "Rachel."

The drumbeat rose to one hundred sixty beats per minute, then dropped to one hundred nine. That made me nervous. "The baby will be here by noon," the doctor predicted.

Then suddenly it was time to move to the delivery room and off we went, bed and all. I soon saw the baby's head crowning, covered with dark hair, and moments later the whole head appeared. Before I could ask what the collar was around the baby's neck, the doctor had clamped and cut it — the umbilical cord. Once freed, my granddaughter made her debut — kicking, screaming, sucking life. Angie whisked her away. I thanked God my two girls were okay.

They named this tiny, doll-like baby Rachel. At 4 pounds 15 ½ ounces, she was one-half ounce lighter than her aunt Christy had been. To me Rachel's birth filled the hollow carved in my heart by the hurt of Christy's death twenty years earlier when, as a poet aptly put it, our rose bloomed beyond the wall.

Life is like that. Daily hurts — big ones and little ones — carve hollows into our hearts as we experience pain and sadness. But sooner or later life's serendipities fill those hollows. Something comes along, something that might have slipped by unnoticed if the hollow had not been there to catch it, something we might have taken for granted. When that happens we experience joy in the same measure we experienced sadness. I thank God that Rachel, now a beautiful young woman, and four other grandchildren fill that hollow in my heart.

~ Shirley G. Brosius

It is only with the heart that one can see rightly.
What is essential is invisible to the eye.

Antoine de Saint Exupéry, *The Little Prince*

30
The House That God Built

As soon as I arrived at Margie's house, I knew something was terribly wrong. It wasn't that anyone was yelling, or crying, or hurt. In fact, outwardly all appeared perfectly normal. Still, I was filled with dread and all I wanted was to go home.

I was twe;ve years old and for several weeks had anticipated this visit to my new friend's house. Margie was the first friend I'd made at my new school, a private school in Hockessin, Delaware. Like many of the students, she lived over the nearby state line in Pennsylvania but didn't want to enroll as a boarding student. So she and her brothers were driven to school every day by their older sister, also a student.

Margie had what I wanted — a big old farmhouse situated on acres and acres of rolling countryside. That was my dream home. I, on the other hand, lived in an oh-so-boring middle-class neighborhood with typical suburban houses plopped down on half-acre lots. To make matters worse, Highway 41 ran right behind our property, and day and night we never got away from the sounds of eighteen-wheelers hauling their heavy loads toward the Delaware-Pennsylvania line.

I couldn't wait to get to Margie's where it would be quiet and peaceful and we could hike her property for hours without ever running into anyone else. Just me, my friend, and nature.

So I didn't understand my feeling when I stepped into the house. Why was I suddenly gripped by fear? Why did I want to run back to my own home where I knew I was, well…*safe*? I had stayed at the homes of many friends and had loved every minute of those visits. Never had I experienced anything like this.

The hours dragged by. Finally the weekend was over and I was driven home again. I remember walking into my house and looking at my mother with an overwhelming sense of relief and love and thankfulness. Dad was home too, and my sisters, and the dog, and my little room was there waiting for me, and in that remarkable moment this unremarkable house on the edge of a highway was — to this kid, at least — the most wonderful place in the world.

I returned to Margie's house several more times over the next few years and each time I had the same strange reaction. I even occasionally pretended to be sick so I could go home early. None of it made sense and yet I couldn't deny what I felt.

When we were about fifteen, Margie invited another friend of hers to spend the weekend and go to an amusement park with us. During that day at the park, Susan and I discovered we were both Christians. When we had a moment alone together, Susan confided to me, "Whenever I go to Margie's house, I claim the blood of Jesus over me."

What a strange thing to say! I'm sure I frowned and shook my head. "Why would you do that?"

"Her sister practices witchcraft," Susan said. "She casts spells and holds séances in the house."

Hearing those words, I finally understood.

I was accustomed to living in a house where God was central to our lives. The Lord was welcome in our home and quite literally dwelt among us. Throughout my growing up years, I was nurtured by his love and undergirded by a sense of security that remains with me today. That strong sense of God's goodness in our home is my sweetest childhood memory.

~ *Ann Tatlock*

31
God Hasn't Given Me a Daddy Yet

Cissy and I had been running around all morning, feverishly trying to get everything we needed to transform my four-year-old bug-and-mud-puddle-loving child into a princess worthy of fairytale fame. It all had to be done by noon because, at that precise hour, my little tomboy princess would be making her grand debut as the flower girl in the wedding of one of her Sunday school teachers.

I was honored that Nikki and Tom had asked my daughter to play a role in their special day, but by the time we got to the beauty parlor for the up-do on her hair, I welcomed the chance to sit down and relax a bit while Lori, a brave and patient beautician, began to take on the challenge of making something particularly elegant out of my daughter's typically pigtailed flyaway hair.

I sat glancing nonchalantly through a magazine, occasionally lending the instinctive mother's ear and eye to what was going on with my daughter. I heard something amidst a conversation between the beautician and Cissy that made me feel proud of my daughter but ashamed of myself.

Lori was nearly finished with Cissy's hair, and as she applied the final ten coats of industrial strength, not-even-a-monsoon-could-move-this-hairdo hairspray to my little girl's beautiful, prom-worthy up-do, she asked Cissy, "What does your daddy say when you come home looking this pretty?"

There are those regretful moments when a single mom gets a sick guilty feeling, knowing that her child is suffering some distress because of her foolish behavior and poor decisions in the past. For me, that was one of those moments.

I had to grit my teeth as I waited to see how Cissy would answer. After all, she never had a daddy and certainly didn't have one at home to admire her hairdo.

She sat there for a second, looking both elegant and childish. She glanced at Lori with all the thoughtfulness a four-year-old child could muster and said, "God hasn't given me a daddy yet."

The one word in Cissy's answer that caught my attention the most was a small one with a big meaning: yet. In that small word, my daughter illustrated a great deal of faith. The certainty and contentment in her voice was a testimony of her faith in a God who loves her and provides for her needs when the time is right.

Perhaps we can all take a lesson from the little word *yet*. We can find it throughout the Bible, and spoken often by Jesus, as an indication of something that is certain to happen eventually. John 7 tells the story prior to the crucifixion and resurrection. Jesus tells his friends and acquaintances that his hour has not *yet* come and he was not *yet* glorified. In John 20, we read that he had not *yet* ascended to his father. In Revelation 8 we hear of trumpets *yet* to sound.

We can know, with an unfailing faithful certainty, that what God tells us is *yet* to come either did happen as promised or will happen when he deems the time is right. Maybe, just maybe, if we adults could attach a *yet* to our so-far-unanswered prayers, the way my daughter and so many small children do, we could live happier, knowing that all of our *yets* are in the Lord's hands after all. And, just like the reliant faith of a child, we should be content to leave them there.

- Autumn Conley

32
Foot-in-the Mouth Problem

The communication gap begins early and is definitely one-sided. Children can say anything and we are supposed to decipher it; however, parents must watch and weigh each word carefully.

Lori, our oldest, came home from kindergarten reciting, "ahh... buh.. cuh.. duh... eh... fuh... guh... huh..." instead of plain ol' A-B-C." The first word she learned to spell was Bobby, "Buh...o...buh...buh...yuh."

I went through that phase until I felt like I knew two languages. We played the darling little sound games of, "Guess what starts with mmmm?" The answer would of course be "mommy, milk, mud, etc."

Naturally, our preschooler, Lisa, wanted to join in. "What begins with brrrr?" she asked. After guessing everything from "bride to "breakdown" I gave up.

With great glee at having stumped her mommy, she informed me, "The word is fire."

"Honey, fire doesn't start with brrrr."

"Well, it does!" she answered indignantly. "Fire burns and burn starts with brrrr."

I don't know if that's early phonetics training or just that children have a natural desire to harass their parents, but there seems no way to get through to them with ordinary, everyday English, especially when they take you literally.

For instance, the children had been particularly rowdy at the dinner table.

"Lori," I said. "If you have finished eating, you may leave the table."

She got up, took her chair to the next room, returned for the pots and pans, then tried to shove the refrigerator through the doorway.

"What in the world are you doing?" I asked, after getting back the voice I had lost when the food lodged in my throat.

She shrugged indifferently. "Well, you said leave the table, so I assumed you wanted me to take everything else."

Later that evening, I was in the bathroom brushing my teeth, when pajama-bottomed David appeared in the doorway.

The thunder was booming and lightning flashing as he ordered, "Would you get out? I have to use the bathroom."

"In a minute," I replied. "Just wait outside."

Realizing my mistake, I had to rush, but caught him just as he stepped onto the front porch.

As parents we like to think we have the final word when things get too far out of hand. Once in a while our children came out with unpleasant, forbidden words.

My mother always said that dirty words required the mouth being washed out with soap. I could never bring myself to go near a child's mouth with soap, but I did threaten to if they didn't do it themselves. I supervised while the child took a washcloth, rubbed a little soap on it and put it on the tongue, then rinsed out the mouth.

"Now, let's have no more dirty little mouths," I admonished.

"There are worse things," Lori retorted. "Some people have ho-hum mouths."

Sending them to their rooms proved to be rather effective discipline. Until one inevitable day! They had been repeatedly warned about misbehaving at the table. Finally, I said, "All right! Go to your rooms as soon as you're finished and lie on your beds."

"Can we play games?" they asked.

"No!" I replied firmly. "You will do nothing but lie on your bed."

They were silent for a moment. Silences can be very dangerous!

They ate their meal hurriedly, small giggles escaping ever so often and a glimmer of mischief traveled around the table from eye to eye.

Like sweet, obedient children, they soon left the table and paraded, one behind the other, down the hallway. Soon, I heard a sentence, then a giggle, another sentence from another one, another giggle.

I knew it was going too well. Before long, they came out. Lisa said, "Mom, I lied three times on my bed. I said, "Lori is pretty. She's not spoiled rotten. And David is a nice brother."

Lori chimed in, "Since I'm older, I lied four times."

"Me too," mimicked little David.

Then Lori added, "I think we've lied enough, so can we stay up now?"

Once they got the grin started on my face, we all knew who had the upper hand — and it wasn't Mommy.

Sometimes it might be wise not to use the correct English word "lie"...but not in this case. I'd be afraid to say "lay" on your bed. I can just see the eggs... and the chickens!

Then there are times when we say, "Get your feet off the table."

They do...and put them back.

"Didn't I tell you...?"

"You said, 'get them off,' not 'keep them off.'"

Although I was expecting my fourth child, things calmed down some after the second child started to kindergarten. She's the one who had come inside one day with her mouth all puckered up, announcing, "Phew! Worms don't taste good." Now, she began practicing her "aah...buh...cuh's" daily and counting for weeks in order to impress her teachers with her knowledge.

But she came home after the first day terribly disappointed. She hadn't learned a thing.

"Are you planning to be a kindergarten dropout?" I asked.

"No," she replied determinedly. "I'm going to keep going 'til I learn something. Then I'm going to quit."

A whole week passed and she still had learned nothing. She said the children wouldn't be quiet and one boy spent his days sitting in the trash can.

The following week on Tuesday she proudly proclaimed, "Today we learned something."

"What did you learn?" I asked eagerly, so glad my bright child wasn't bored anymore. Her education had begun.

"Well," she said slowly, "We learned how to keep our mouths shut."

Oh, Wow! I thought. Wouldn't it be grand to have such a kindergarten for adults. Then perhaps I could come close to the "ideal woman" presented in Proverbs 31. Particularly verse 26-28: *When she speaks, her words are wise, and kindness is the rule when she gives instruction. She carefully watches all that goes on in her household and does not have to bear the consequences of laziness. Her children stand and bless her. Her husband praises her.*

My problem isn't caused by phonetics or childlike thinking. I say things that are understood all too well.

But...in my day, the school had no kindergarten. We just jumped right into the first grade.

I wonder if the Lord is going to say that's good enough excuse for my all-too-often foot-in-mouth disease?

~ Yvonne Lehman

33
This I Know

My friend Kathy loved horses and wanted to use them to help children. When she opened a therapeutic riding center, she knew she had found the ministry she'd always dreamed of. Using horses to help physically and mentally challenged children, she witnessed many miracles. But one in particular always stood out in her mind.

Ryan was three when his parents first brought him for treatment. Like most autistic children, Ryan could not connect with the world around him. He rarely spoke, never more than one or two words, and didn't like to be touched. To calm himself, he spun in circles

At Ryan's first session, Kathy introduced the preschooler to Billy, a gentle quarter horse. As the mount stood quietly at the edge of the ring, Kathy placed Ryan's hand on the big horse's flank and said, "This is Billy. He'll be your friend." Ryan gave no indication that he heard.

When volunteers tried to seat Ryan on Billy's back, Ryan began screaming. Down on the ground again, he became a whirling top, churning up the sawdust and making it clear there was no way he was going to get on that horse.

"Sonia, sit behind Ryan and hold him tightly," Karen told a teen assistant and firmly placed Ryan in the saddle. Walkers on each side stood ready to catch a flying child should the need arise.

Ryan continued to scream, but as Sonia hung on, the three-year-old began to relax. When the horse started walking, the movement caught the boy off guard, and Kathy saw a flicker of curiosity.

Ear-splitting screams initiated the second riding session, but this time Kathy decided to try a different tack. As Sonia closely held a squirming, screeching Ryan atop Billy, Kathy began to sing to him. Like many autistic children, Ryan responded to music by calming down, so Kathy sang all the children's Sunday school songs she could think of. "Jesus Loves Me" seemed to be his favorite.

"Slowly slide down from the horse," Kathy whispered to Sonia, when she drew a breath between songs. Oblivious of the change, Ryan rode by himself for the rest of the session, listening while Kathy and the volunteers took turns singing.

Hoping for a breakthrough, Kathy was disappointed as week after week proved to be the same. Ryan remained completely uncooperative when a physical therapist attempted to work with him. Soothing the three-year-old with repeated choruses of "Jesus loves me, this I know" and leading him around the arena on Billy seemed the best they could accomplish. Kathy could see no signs that they were getting through Ryan's tough mental barriers.

Then one day six weeks later, Kathy walked beside Billy and held up a plastic ring within Ryan's reach, just as she had done many times before. "Take the ring from my hand, Ryan," she instructed.

And he did. Surprised, Kathy held up another. Ryan took it too.

From that moment, Ryan's participation escalated. He would pick a ring from the therapist's hand and hold it as volunteers led Billy to a corner of the arena where Ryan slipped the ring onto a pole. Over the next several months, he began choosing rings of a particular color when directed and responding to other simple requests.

Despite Ryan's improvements in cooperating with the therapists, however, there were still no signs of social interaction, no connection with the people around him or even the horse beneath him. Ryan stared straight ahead, his actions mechanical and robotic in nature. He neither spoke nor smiled. When frustrated, he withdrew further and regressed to his old custom of twirling in circles. His parents reported little change in behavior at home.

When Kathy saw no real improvement after ten months of weekly sessions, she began to wonder if they were raising false expectations for Ryan's parents. She knew if she could see one spark of curiosity like she did that first day he rode Billy, she could justify continued treatment.

Shortly thereafter, on a bright spring afternoon, Kathy took Ryan for a ride along the new trail volunteers had constructed to appeal to the riders' five senses. The youngster blinked when they led him out the barn doors into the dazzling sunshine. As Ryan rode up and down the trail's hills, he seemed increasingly fascinated with the sights and sounds that bombarded him. He looked up at birds singing in the trees and reached for colorful pool noodles strung across his path. He listened to the different tones a set of chimes made as he struck them with a mallet Kathy handed him. He felt inside a mailbox to retrieve a hidden object. Pleased with Ryan's progress, Kathy led Billy back toward the barn.

What happened next made her heart stop.

As they moved from the bright sunshine into the darkness of the arena, Ryan looked down at Kathy and for the first time, made eye contact. Then he made eye contact with the side-walker. Ryan stared at Billy's neck in front of him and turned around to look at his tail, suddenly seeming to realize he sat on a horse.

"Nobody move," Kathy told the volunteers. "I want complete silence."

Kathy led Billy around for twenty minutes more while Ryan focused on different objects in the arena as if he had never seen them before. When Kathy finally took Ryan down from the saddle, she paused a moment with him in her arms. Then, with determination, she walked over and set him on his mother's lap. Ryan snuggled close. For the first time since Ryan was born, his young mother was able to hold and cuddle her little boy. She sat on the deck for forty-five minutes and cried as she rocked him.

"You sit there as long as you want," said Kathy, wiping away her own tears.

On the way home that afternoon, Ryan's mother pulled over to the side of the highway and called Kathy's number. She was crying so hard she could barely talk. "Kathy, you have to hear this," she said, sobbing into her cell phone.

From the back seat came a tiny voice, singing, "Je-sus loves me, this I know."

- Tracy Crump

34
A Mother's Heart

With my fortieth birthday approaching this year, I have to admit that I am struggling with this milestone. I have had a variety of responses to this struggle from friends, everything from "I struggled also" to "it's no big deal, get over it."

I don't have to do much soul searching to realize why this is such an issue for me. Since I was a little girl, all I ever wanted was to be a wife and mother. This is a hope and dream that I have continuously prayed about and hoped for since that time.

Unfortunately, it is a dream that has not come to fruition.

There have been times when I have really struggled with this unfulfilled dream. One of my most challenging times was after I left an abusive marriage. During this trying time in my life, I was happy for my sister and a close friend, both of whom were expecting their second child. However, the green-eyed monster ate away at me for months. I was filled with anger and venom, because they had what I have always wanted. I had to work through this with continuous prayer and reminding myself of the deep love I have for these precious people in my life.

There are solutions for a single woman wanting children today, but for a variety of reasons these options either do not feel right or are not feasible for me. All I can do is continue to pray and pour my heart out to God. Proverbs 3:5-6 tells me: *Lean on, trust in, and be confident in the Lord with all your heart and mind and do not rely on your own insight or understanding. In all your ways know, recognize, and acknowledge Him, and He will direct and make straight and plain your paths.* (AMP)

Sometimes I wonder if God hears my prayers or why I've had to wait for so long. For over a decade I have prayed the prayer of Hannah found in the first chapter of 1 Samuel. I have referred to my desired children specifically by name. There are times when God reminds me that although he has not directly answered my prayer and allowed me to give birth to and raise a child of my own, he has allowed my mother's heart to serve and minister for him.

I can see this service throughout many periods of my life:

First, I am a decade older than my sister and brother. They have always been my babies. I took them under my wing, and although my parents did not ask me to, I mothered them from the beginning. Even though they are now grown with families of their own, they are still my babies. I love my niece and nephews and dote on them to the point that I joke with Mama that they are both her and my grandchildren.

Second, for over two decades I have actively cared in various capacities for my aging grandparents, who have lived into their nineties. With their aging the roles have been reversed and I have taken on the role of parent.

Third, I have worked with children and young people in a variety of capacities over the years through teaching and church work.

Fourth, returning to school as an adult student I became close with a group of young people who I mentored. Sometimes these young adults just needed a listening ear, friendly smile and loving heart.

Fifth, I work in the activities department at a local nursing home. I love my 80+ residents. They have a wide range of needs and abilities. Some are dementia and Alzheimer's patients who are deeply lost in the disease. God reminds me continuously that this is a ministry. Daily, the residents bless me just as much as I am allowed to bless them. I also am an advocate for my residents. I realized just how protective I am of their needs and wants when another staff member questioned the fact my residents are given ice cream once a week. I became a mother bear fiercely protecting her cubs.

These opportunities remind me of the servant heart and attitude of Mother Theresa. She said, "Give yourself fully to God. He will use you to accomplish great things on the condition that you believe much more in his love than in your own weakness." Her life of service should be a model for others.

> I don't know if my desire to have a child of my own will ever grow to fruition. However, when I take the time to look, I see how God has used my mother's heart to allow me to help minister and serve others. Only God knows the reasons for

this and the impact I have made on those I have been allowed to mother over the years. I am reminded of Proverbs 16:9. *A man's mind plans his way, but the Lord directs his steps and makes them sure.*

In the meantime, I'll continue to pray and seek God's will for my life. He reminds us in Ecclesiastes 3 that "for everything there is a season." Although the desire to be a mother has intensified over the years, God promises that he will sustain me and give me the strength for whatever the future may hold and in whatever capacity he decides to use this mother's heart.

~ Diana Leagh Matthews

"I assure you, when you did it to one of the least of these my brothers and sisters, you were doing it to me!"
Jesus (Matthew 25:40 NLT)

35

I Am

I am an ordinary girl with a talent for swimming
   who can't stand that my Grandfather's gone.
I wonder if he likes his new life in Heaven.
I hear him singing "Mary don't you know," his favorite song.

I see him cooking breakfast for me.
I want him to come back to life.
I am an ordinary girl with a talent for swimming
   who can't stand that my Grandfather's gone.

I pretend that I'm fine but sometimes I'm not.
I feel that he's here but I can't see him.
I touch his picture and remember everything.
I worry if I'll ever get over his death.
I cry when I lay flowers on his grave.
I am an ordinary girl with a talent for swimming
   who can't stand that my Grandfather's gone.

I understand that he's not coming back.
I say I'm fine, but it's not true.
I dream that he's here.
I try not to cry about him.
I hope I see him again.
I am an ordinary girl with a talent for swimming
   who can't stand that my Grandfather's gone.

- Emily Marett

36
The Potholder

The first time I remember praying on my own was when I was a little girl. My family and I had plans to go to the lake for a summer swim and picnic. I was sitting on the living room sofa — wearing a bathing suit with ruffles in the back, my colorful inner tube around my waist so I could float in the water without fear of drowning — patiently waiting for family members to get ready for our outing. As the sky turned from blue to gray, I heard Mother say, "It looks like it's going to rain. We may have to go to the lake another day."

When the raindrops began to fall, so did my child's beating heart. I began to pray. "God, I really want to go to the lake today, but if it rains, we can't go. Please stop the rain God. Please stop the rain. I can't wait for another sunny day to swim."

Within about five minutes, the rain eased before totally stopping. Imagine how surprised I was, thinking God had answered a child's prayer! I was elated, just thinking that God would stop the rain. With one prayer. For one child. I treasured that special moment and never told one soul for fear I would be ridiculed.

Eventually, my wonderment about that rainy day subsided. I realized that summer showers were sporadic and some stopped as quickly as they started. What I'd experienced wasn't so special after all, more than likely.

The incident no longer seemed as special, though I often wondered if God really did stop the rain for me. He never answered in one way or another. So there were times I would forget about God. Times I would forget to pray until the next time I went back to church. It was hard for me to have a conversation with a God who didn't talk back to a little child when she talked to him. Sometimes I forgot he even existed.

Until one day. I was outside sitting on my front porch making potholders. Someone had given me a metal loom with a bag of cotton loops and I had great fun making potholders and giving them to my mother, family, and friends. I made yellow and green potholders, and potholders that were blue and red. Some I made blue and yellow. When down to my last loops, I noticed the only colors left were blue and green. thought a blue and green potholder would be the ugliest potholder ever made.

But then, my attention was suddenly drawn to the blue sky above. It was a gorgeous day with a few big fat fluffy clouds floating by — a day when bluebirds fly high and redbirds fluff their wings. As I looked at the sky, I noticed the green leaves of a tall tree and then lower, green grass that grew up to meet the azure. It was then I heard God whisper into my spirit, "See, blue and green do look good together. I made the grass and leaves green so the color would be a pleasant color that would be easy for the eyes to look at for long periods of time without tiring. And the blue of the sky where it touches the trees is such a soft blue, the color fades to gentle the greeting of the two colors when they meet."

I knew without a doubt that I had heard God's whisper. I could hear him talking to me. Not in an audible voice. But somehow in my head and mind, somehow deep inside of me, he spoke to teach me. It was as though he'd cupped my chin and turned my face to look at the sky and trees as he shared with me about his beautiful creation.

And the blue and green potholder? I thought it so pretty I decided to give it to my Aunt Inez, an aunt who sometimes let me stay with her. An aunt who loved and cherished me and, in the future, would love my own children.

Many years later, after Aunt Inez had passed through the veil to return Home, I made another blue and green potholder. This one was for me, to be a constant reminder not only of God's blue skies and green leaves and grass — his creation — but that I am a pot he's fashioned so the Holy Spirit can be my teacher and comforter while God's Son Jesus is my savior, intercessor, and holder for eternity, the magnificent and awesome pot holder of my soul. The Christ who helps me and holds me forever and since he considers me his bride, the One and Only who will always cherish me and never let me go — even on rainy days.

~ *Vicki H. Moss*

I am not afraid of storms for I am learning how to sail my ship.
Louisa May Alcott, *Little Women*

37

Joni

Many years ago when my teaching career was just beginning, I was anxious about the opening day of school with a new group of first graders. It was important for me to feel that I had chosen the right vocation where I could touch lives and make a difference in the world along with bringing home an income.

As the students arrived, some were escorted by mothers who were anxious about who the new teacher would be and the kind of person who would have the care of their child in the classroom. Some children were shy, a few couldn't stand still, and others were outspoken and demanding.

I saw the beauty in each of them. They were little bundles of potential and it was my duty to inspire them to love school and to unleash their desire to learn.

Insecurities about my own ability to be the amazing teacher I wanted to be crept into my thoughts from time to time.

I could hardly wait from day to day to see what cute things the students would do and say. First graders are endearing in that way. Out of innocence and misunderstanding they say and do memorable things. Particularly impressive was Joni, a pretty little girl with brown hair, freckles and big blue eyes.

On one of the early days of school Joni said, "I love to ride the bus to school with the big kids. It makes me feel important."

Those words created a whole new awareness for me about how small children see themselves in relation to older children.

Another time, she wore new black patent leather shoes with lacy anklets. She kept watching her feet all day, poking behind the rest of the class, taking her slow sweet time when her turn came for the bathroom, and so on. I assumed she loved the way her new shoes and fancy socks looked.

But I had missed the point altogether. She said, "I love the way my new shoes sound when I walk. I can hear every step."

She had been counting her steps and listening for footfalls to call out the numbers in her head. Every step was important.

First grade faculty members rotated morning bus duty and made sure the buses were unloaded safely and completely at the designated drop-off area at the end of the school. The bus driver had the students leave in an orderly manner and older children had a tendency to watch out for the younger ones, especially if they had siblings on the bus with them. Joni always stopped at the bottom of the stairs and turned to say something to bus driver.

Her farewells were a variety of partings. She would say, "Have a nice day," or "Thank you for driving us to school today," or "You are the best bus driver ever."

One morning she looked up at me and said, "I love riding the bus to school, and I can go up and down those big stairs all by myself."

The key thing that set Joni apart was that she loved life. She loved people. She loved every new experience and had the gift of finding something new to love on a daily basis. Life never got boring for her. Even in the daily routines, she discovered all sorts of new things to adore.

One day Joni's mother let her wear the pale yellow dress with layers of crinoline that had been picked out for Easter Sunday church service the previous weekend. She spun around in circles all day whenever she had a reason to be out of her seat. She looked like a dancing daffodil twirling about. I had to tell her to get back in her seat more than once.

"I love my new dress," she told me.

"It is very pretty," I assured her.

"When I'm spinning around, I feel just like a fairy princess," she declared. She spun around again to show me how full her skirt became when filled with the motion of spinning. "I wish I could spin forever."

I wish I had kept notes on all the lovely and precious things children told me over the years. Now retired after a full career in the classroom, I still remember lessons I learned from my students.

I taught Joni and her classmates how to read, write, and do math problems, but they also taught me life lessons. Every child was not only a learner, but a teacher to a listening adult.

In particular Joni taught me that there is something new and exciting to appreciate every day and attitude makes all the difference. Perhaps most important was that she taught me to see the world through the eyes of a child and to allow time in my teaching day to discover the unique personality of each student who walked through the doors of my classroom.

~ Judith Victoria Hensley

He who teaches children learns more than they do.
German Proverb

38
Can't Live Here Anymore

"I can't live here any more," four-year-old Laurie declared.

"I'm sorry you feel that way," I replied, wondering what prompted her statement. Before I could ask, she continued. "I'm almost five. We always have quiet time after lunch and I don't want to do that any more."

"Quiet time is good for all of us, Honey," I explained. "You have library books to read or you can listen to your records."

She shook her head. "I don't want to, Mama, so I can't live here any more."

Laurie set out for the house next door, where her arrival caught my neighbor, Joyce, by surprise. Joyce gently guided Laurie back home, explaining that she already had two children and no extra bedroom. Waiting for her in the front yard, I tried to hug my distraught daughter.

She wasn't in a hugging mood.

"Since Joyce didn't have room, maybe you could wait and tell Daddy how you feel," I said in an effort to dissuade her. "He'll be home for lunch soon. If you leave before he comes, he will really miss you."

Laurie tossed her long, brown curls and looked at me with her big blue eyes. "Daddy will just tell me the same as you. And I don't want to have quiet time."

It was apparent she was not going to give in. She would go live with her four friends two houses away. She stopped only long enough to say a tearful farewell to the little maple tree she and her daddy had planted recently. Then, without a backward glance, she ran away to her new life.

After making sure Laurie arrived safely at my neighbor's house, I dashed in to call Jo.

"Laurie is in your yard," I told her, "but she's not there just to play. She's planning to move in with you. She's protesting the afternoon quiet hour." I gave Jo a minute to digest that news. Then she asked what we should do.

"What do you mean, what should we do?" I said. "You have four kids. Hasn't one of them ever tried to run away?"

"No." Jo laughed. "My children are very happy here."

With Laurie at her door, Jo and I had no time to discuss a plan. We simply agreed to wing it.

Just as I hung up the phone, Clair arrived for lunch. He received a hug and kiss from three-year-old Nancy who was already sitting at the table.

"Laurie ran away," Nancy announced.

After I gave him a brief summation he walked over to Jo's house, positive Laurie would come home with him if he went to get her. He soon returned — minus the runaway, and obviously dejected. "She told me she doesn't live here any more."

I assured him that our daughter would end her protest and return home when she discovered Jo had the same rule about quiet time.

Clair went back to work. Nancy and I read a story from one of her Golden books before she took her nap. I was confident Jo would call any minute to say Laurie was on her way home.

When Jo did call, it was not the news I was expecting. After they finished lunch, Jo explained to Laurie there were no extra beds in the children's rooms, so unfortunately she would have to lie on the floor.

"I told her I was sorry I could only give her a blanket. I suggested maybe she would rather return home where she could have her own bed in her own room," Jo said. "She just took the blanket and went to Janine's bedroom."

After Nancy awoke from her nap, I left her with Joyce, the neighbor who had been Laurie's first choice. I gathered two of Laurie's favorite possessions — Racky, her stuffed red raccoon, and her satin-edged blue blanket tattered from years of stroking. Then I walked down to Laurie's new place of residence.

"Hi Carolyn, come in." Jo greeted me, loud enough for the children to hear from their rooms down the hallway. "It looks like you brought something with you."

Speaking equally loud, I began to explain about Racky and the blanket when Laurie appeared.

"Hi, Mama," she said smiling. "I really like living here."

"That's good," I said. "I want you to be happy because I love you. However, Daddy and I have a problem and we need your help."

I waited long enough to pique her curiosity and make sure she had seen Racky and her blue blanket.

"Now that you're big enough to leave home," I continued, "there is an extra bed. We're not sure what to do with it and all your clothes and toys. Nancy can wear your clothes some day, but she doesn't need your bed or toys because she has her own. Anyway, they would make her sad because they would be a reminder that you don't live with us any more. Since the bed and toys are yours, we thought you should be the one to decide what to do with them."

I paused for a moment and adjusted Racky on my lap to call attention to him.

"You always like it when we help our missionaries," I said. "Maybe there's a little girl in one of our missionary families who would like to have your things — especially your toys."

With each word, Laurie's smile faded. Tears quickly followed. She ran to me and climbed onto my lap.

"Oh, Mama," she wailed. "I don't really like living here. There's a big clown balloon in the bedroom and I have to lie on the floor and it's hard and I miss Daddy and Nancy and you and I don't want you to give away my things. I want to keep Racky and my blanket and live at my own house again. I don't care if I have to do quiet hour." She buried her face in my shoulder and sobbed.

Jo and I winked discreetly while I comforted Laurie. I assured her that having her come home was exactly what we hoped she would decide. I wiped away her tears and tucked the blue blanket in one of her arms. Laurie's other arm wrapped around Racky's neck as she kissed him on his long turned-up nose. Giving Jo an appreciative glance, I took Racky, the blue blanket and my runaway home.

The next day at lunch, Nancy pondered her sister's adventure.

"I might run away too," she declared, her blonde ponytail swirling as she bobbed her head.

"You better not," admonished her now-much-wiser sister. "It's not as much fun as you think it is."

~ *Carolyn Barnum*

39

Comparisons

She bounds down the concrete steps, two or three at a time, with a big smile on her face. She is covered with dry dirt — her hair, face, arms, legs, shoes. I know which sundress she has on, but I still can't tell what color it's supposed to be. Everything is covered with, at the very least, a fine layer of red dust. Her grimy socks have been eaten by her sneakers; now they resemble sports socks without the fuzzy pom-poms on the back. Both shoes are untied and in very real danger of leaving her feet. Her hair is wild — part of it is matted and part is flying all over the place. She is hollering "Hi, Mama!" over and over and is squirmy with excitement. She runs down the line of a few cars and jumps into ours, obviously glad to see me.

A few steps behind her, another little girl starts down those concrete steps. She is immaculate in a pale pink blouse with matching slacks. There is not a speck of dirt anywhere on this child's clothes or body. Her blouse is neatly tucked in and a slim maroon belt encircles her slender waist. She wears a pretty necklace made of big pink and white beads. Her hair is fixed into two identical pigtails — every hair is where it is supposed to be and the pigtails are exactly in the same place on each side of her head. She carefully makes her way down each step, one at a time, occasionally glancing at her waiting mother with a demure smile.

While my child is launching into a manic monologue about her day, her spotless friend quietly greets her mother and gracefully seats herself in the car.

On our way home, while my excited little chatterbox continues in minute detail, I think about the complete femininity of my daughter's friend. I have never compared my rough little tomboy with anyone else for any reason, but the difference in these two girls strikes me with a surprising force.

I glance at my perfectly formed, smart-as-a-whip, cute-as-a-button daughter and wonder if I should be treating her differently so that she would be more feminine. Perhaps I should have given her more dolls and tea sets. Maybe I should have forbidden her to play with big brother's cars and trucks in the sandbox. I'm sure dressing her in his hand-me-downs much of the time doesn't help, either.

I look at her again and feel lucky to have a child so full of life and love. But is it luck? "No," a voice inside me says. "God gave you this child to love and nurture, and that's what you are doing. Let her be herself."

When we stop at the next corner, I impulsively give her a tight hug. A small cloud of red dust rises around her head, and from somewhere on that dirty, dirty face, a smile beams out at me as I hear her say, "I love you, Mama."

- Carol Weeks

There are only two lasting bequests we can hope to give our children.
One is roots; the other, wings.
~ Hodding Carter

40
My Best Name

I'll never forget the day Leonard, my adoption worker, sat across the table and announced he had a baby girl for me. I had waited eleven months, longer than being pregnant, for this moment. The Humpty Dumpty wallpaper was hung, the curtains made, the crib purchased and assembled. I had picked a name.

"Her name is Linda," Leonard continued. "I encourage you to name her anything you'd like. It will help you bond with her and form a strong connection. She is nine months old. She will never remember Linda."

The next day, a typical San Diego summer day, a cool breeze blew off the ocean and wispy white clouds headed swiftly west across the sky. I went to meet my baby. Her foster mother had dressed her in a soft blue smocked dress and black patent leather shoes. Her clean skin glowed. Her brown eyes were the color of chestnuts. At first, I watched her play with toys through a two-way mirror.

"If for any reason, you don't want her just say so," Leonard prompted. "And you can take a few days to think it over if you would like."

Did he really think I could say no to that sweet, gorgeous child? She was mine. The next day we began our "forever" life for better or for worse, through sickness and in health, 'til death us do part.

Growing up in San Diego County, I knew Linda was the Spanish word meaning beautiful. It was a good name, but not the name I had chosen.

I had searched through many reference books and studied names. I tried out some pretty strange combinations, like "Nova Caprice." A friend asked, "Are you adopting a Chevrolet or a baby?" "Patience?" Well, what if she's not? I finally settled on a name with family significance and religious meaning. My mother, of Jewish decent, was named Betty. Betty means my God is an oath. Tina means follower of Christ. Both names, Betty and Tina, are of Jewish/Hebrew origin. If ever there was a follower of Christ, it was my mother. My daughter's name would be Bettina, "Tina."

The decision made, I never gave serious consideration to Linda.

Tina's birth certificate was amended, her adoption finalized — she was Tina. She was also very beautiful. Her birth mother had, no doubt, seen that when she named her Linda. I did not regret changing her name. It was, as Leonard said, good for our bond.

When Tina was three, we moved to Placerville, California in the Sierra Foothills. To help us adjust to our new home and form relationships, I enrolled Tina in a twice-weekly playgroup. I was a stay at home mom, so we had the opportunity to participate in various community activities. Bible study, children's hour at the library, gymnastics and swimming lessons became part of our weekly routine.

We were both making friends. I had an assortment of friends. *All* of Tina's friends were named Linda. The favorite adult in her life was her gymnastics coach, Linda. Her best friend, at playgroup, was Linda. I noticed — but she didn't seem to.

At age five, Tina started school. Her first school friend, Linda, is the same Linda who remains her best adult friend. If there was more than one Linda in her class, she had more than one best friend. She began telling me, "My best," meaning her favorite, "name is Linda." I heard this dozens, probably hundreds of times. I knew Leonard had been wrong. She did remember! I had made a mistake when I changed her name.

Tina went from saying, "My best name is Linda," to "Why didn't you name me Linda? You know, Linda is my best name." I would nod, but not answer. I grieved for the little girl who had lost her name. What had I done to my child? Her distress over her name was obvious. I loved her unconditionally. Still, I did not know how to fix the problem I had caused.

At eight, Tina became more obsessed with the name Linda. It was clear to me her name change was a huge concern. I became anxious it might be turning into a psychological issue.

In Bible study, I read Jesus' words in John 8:32, "*Then you will know the truth, and the truth will set you free.*" I would have to tell Tina the truth, someday, when the time was right, when I knew she was ready to hear it and when God gave me the right words.

I picked her up from school one afternoon. After running errands in town, we started snaking our way up the winding mountain road leading to our country home. It was early June. Spring rains had filled Hangtown Creek to the brim. Water rushed over the rocky creek bed making bubbly whitewater rapids and sounding like diesel engines straining to make the grade.

"Mommy, I wish you'd have named me Linda. Linda is my best name." Tina's young remorseful voice pierced my heart. It was time.

I pulled the Jeep Cherokee onto a wide shoulder, set the parking brake, and moved into the back seat. "Tina, I need to tell you, your name was Linda. I changed it. If you want to be Linda, I will turn the car around. We will go to the courthouse right now and change your name back to Linda."

"Why did you name me Tina?"

"I thought you would like to be named after your grandmother. But, I love you. Your name is not important to me. I will love you no matter what name you have. You can choose. If you don't want to choose today and if you choose some other time, that is okay. I'll change your name if you want to."

For a while I waited, hearing only the tumultuous roar of the creek.

While Tina thought quietly, I, too, was thinking. A name is such an important thing. Memory is triggered by hearing your name. When you are in the shopping mall with noisy conversations around, all you hear is babbling until someone says your name. Your name stands out. It rises above the din. It gets your attention. When you are waiting in the doctor's office and the patients are called back one by one, you barely notice. But when the assistant calls your name, the sound transcends your concentration and you know it is your turn. Your name is what sets you apart from the crowd.

I did not bond with Tina's name. I connected with those big eyes and dimpled elbows, the sandy hair and chubby legs. I bonded at the crib side, in the emergency room, in the rocker and the classroom. Our attachment strengthened as our tears ran together and dripped off our chins and when we laughed hysterically at each other's antics. My heart entwined with hers in an awesome way through a miracle of love.

At last Tina spoke. "Tina is okay, but Linda is still my best name. I'll be Tina." Truth did set us free. I never heard about Linda again.

~ Karen R. Hessen

41

The Game

It happened when I was in second grade. Before students were taken to their classrooms for the day, we congregated in the gym. We could work on our homework, talk and maybe play a game.

A game. That's how it began.

A group of us girls sat close together. We were probably bored and had too much time on our hands.

"We could play checkers." I had a small magnetic checkerboard and the black and red metal pieces would cling to it.

"No, we have done that before."

"What about riddley-riddley-ree?"

"No, we do that all the time." Cassie tapped her chin. "How about a new game?"

We were all ears.

A boy sat off to the side, alone. At that age girls and boys hate each other and they have fights and pick on each other. But this boy…we knew he was different from the others. He was big and had some learning difficulties and spoke slowly.

Cassie motioned us closer and whispered, "That boy, he's different. You can't go near him, you can't talk to him. If he comes close, you have to cross your fingers or else you will end up like him."

Our heads nodded in agreement.

We adhered to the rules like a sacred religion. I don't know how long the game lasted. Maybe a few weeks, maybe a few months. Another student heard about what Cassie was doing and told the teacher.

I passed Cassie in the hallway and overheard the teacher reprimanding her. A still-small-voice murmured in my ear, *Tell the truth, Veronica. You are just as guilty!*

I pretended not to hear and kept on walking.

The next morning in the gym, Cassie was made to apologize to the boy and was given detention.

Cassie may have been the ringleader but the rest of us were equal participants. Yet she did not betray us followers and we got off scot-free.

Even as Cassie made her apology, my friend and I hid our hands behind our lunchboxes and crossed our fingers. We swapped devious smiles.

The game was over. As time went by we forgot to cross our fingers and forgot to ignore the boy. I don't know when it occurred to me that I had done wrong but at some point it dawned on me. I felt bad, but not nearly enough to pay for my actions, so I never confessed. The teachers and the other students considered me a good girl to the point that they thought I was perfect. Most of all, I feared what punishments I might receive.

One morning I went into the gym and sat a few feet away from the boy. I hadn't been paying attention, except for noticing that his tennis shoes were muddy and that he had tracked in on the floor.

Cassie looked my way. "Veronica, you don't want to sit there. It's muddy."

The boy dipped his head.

I knew what Cassie really meant. Rather than play along as I had done before, I mumbled, "Leave me alone, Cassie."

The boy and I exchanged a look, but that was all. I never did truly apologize. That was as close as I came to atonement.

Nearly twenty years have passed. Whenever I remember that game I am eaten up with shame and guilt, not just for my behavior, but for never confessing and apologizing to the boy I hurt.

I have come to the conclusion that in this game of life, if we are going to follow anyone, let it be Jesus.

- Veronica Leigh

42

The Common Pot

Vacations were a time we all looked forward to. The children had never seen the ocean so we decided the summer after our move to the mountains would be a good time to take them. It would help occupy their minds with something other than having left their Illinois home for good.

During the five-hour drive, Howard and I launched into vivid descriptions of the ocean, the foam, breakers, shells, sandy beach and the tide that comes in at night and recedes during the morning.

The children could hardly wait. The sky was beautiful blue, dotted with fluffy white clouds that I was daring to rain. (I have my remedy for that! Just get a couple of cardboard boxes, pack away all summer clothes on a high shelf in a closet and the sun is certain to shine. Has never failed! Of course the reverse works too — wash your car and it's sure to rain.)

With dreams of utopia, we were looking forward to the week of no time schedules and children playing, rather than bickering.

The second we stepped out of the car after arriving at the condo, we began to hear four piercing screams. The children were being attacked from the ground.

"Baby porcupines!" one exclaimed.

"Needles!"

"Animals with stingers!"

"Sand burrs," we explained.

They pulled them out and left them there to step on the next time they passed that way.

We were hoping they would run for the beach rather than the television, but the first child inside switched on the TV and raced for a chair, shouting, "This one's mine."

Another jumped on the couch, "I get this."

"Why do they get all the good seats?" another wailed. "Moooommmeeeee!"

"Don't yell at me!" I shouted. "Get your bathing suits on."

Finally, donned in bathing apparel, we headed for the beach. Oh, like music to the ears, those delighted squeals as they stood at the edge of the wave and let the sand wash out from under their feet.

Yet they were reluctant about this new experience, so we urged them not to be afraid, to try it, play, let the water roll over them, jump the waves, stand in the breakers.

Two minutes later I was screaming, "Don't go out too far," and "We've lost one!"

Before long, I was well aware that the only rest and relaxation I was going to get had already taken place — in the car on the drive down, just thinking and talking about the wonderful time we were going to have.

Howard, was most reassuring, relating his war experience when he had almost drowned and had to be pulled out of he ocean, wearing uniform, boots, back pack and military equipment.

But I had brought along a recommended best selling novel to relax with: *Jaws!*

Our youngest would not venture beyond the edge of the water and insisted upon making her sand castles there.

They played until dark. Later, David complained he had a stomachache and couldn't imagine why he, "of all people," had to have a stomachache while on vacation.

I couldn't imagine either! It couldn't possibly be because his plastic surfboard had gone head first into the sand with him balanced on his stomach on the other end while the waves swept over him. He'd hung on to the surfboard for dear life until it broke in the middle. Then he tried to drink the ocean.

At dinner we explained the various seafoods to the children then listened with mortification as they ordered, "grilled cheese, hamburgers, French fries and catsup."

After all the orders arrived we let the children sample our assortment of seafood, hoping for favorable responses. It reminded me of the films I've seen where dinner is eaten from a common pot. You know the ones: The wife cooks the food in one pot, clangs on a triangle, the husband and children run from their work to sit under a shade tree where they all dip into the pot, eating with their fingers, licking them, and all hands go into the pot of food again.

Our little one did like "those French fries with the tails on them."

I had laboriously explained about the tide coming in at night and receding in the morning. Trying to intelligently discuss the moon and its relationship to the tides, I told them that by the time we had finished our late dinner, the entire beach would probably be covered with water.

After dinner we trekked to the beach to see. All eyes were upon me, and a strange grin played about the lips of my hubby. (I think men are born gloaters.)

"What happened to the ocean?" they asked, noting that the beach was twice as large as it had been when we left it earlier. The tide had not come in. It had gone out, and with it, all the opinions that Mommy might know something after all.

"Well," I said bravely, "this is a strange phenomenon. We will research it later."

Howard had to put in his two-cents worth. "There's one thing about Mommy. She might not know everything, but she knows where to go to find out." The children weren't impressed.

Before the week was over, they were having contests to see who could get the most sand burrs in their feet before getting to the beach.

Then they began to collect shells. All the shells!

~ Yvonne Lehman

43
When Faith Flickers

Danika sat at the kitchen table prolonging every bite of her dinner as she often did by singing and swinging her feet. While starting the water for her bath, I yelled at her to hurry up. This was no night to chew every bite a thousand times or hide behind her fork and pretend she was trapped in a tiny prison while peering out and waving at me. We were about to get hit by another storm, and this time I wanted to be ready.

"Do I get to take a bath in a bowl?" Danika asked between bites of macaroni and cheese. Her four-year-old face was smudged and smiling as she no doubt remembered her favorite part of losing power the last time. Obviously this was a fun time for her, but not so much for me as I remembered the complete darkness when I blew out the candles and the overwhelming feeling that I was not totally clean, not to mention the pungent smell of hand sanitizer that followed me throughout the house.

I decided this time I would not be caught off guard and have to bathe my child from bottled water poured into a green plastic bowl again.

"Not this time," I said. "Not if I can help it."

I flipped on the light for the basement and hurried down stairs for the gallons of water I had bought recently, remembering how I'd learned to retrieve water from the hot water tank during the last big storm to use for flushing the toilets. "Not this time," I said again as I hoisted them up the stairs and headed to the bathroom. This time I would have water ready to flush. I felt so proud.

"Come look at the trees, Mommy!" Danika yelled.

Through the doors leading onto the deck I watched as the trees encircling our yard bent over so far I wondered how they didn't all snap. It was as if they were learning to play leapfrog with some imaginary giant who was shoving them into submission. As the wind growled, I cringed and waited for the first tree to snap. I envisioned a sort of domino effect that would leave that surrounding army of trees flattened like a war zone.

The lights began to flicker.

"Finish your milk," I ordered.

I scurried to Danika's room to get her pajamas, underwear, and brush while she finished drinking her milk. I knew it would be easier to gather all of her bedtime things now while I still had the bright lights overheard to direct me. I remembered how hard it was to search for things with a flashlight. Now I was yelling at the lights to stay on when they flickered again.

"Come on we need to hurry!"

Danika's milk moustache glistened as I rushed her into the bathroom. I turned off the water, reminding myself not to pull the plug after she was done (more water to flush with), and strategically positioned a flashlight beside the tub. I knew how far away it was from the wall and the tub, so when the power went out, which would be any minute now, I would be able to find it.

"Can I play?" Danika asked as she sunk her little legs into the water and reached for the plastic mermaid.

"Are you serious?" I asked. "Not tonight!" The lights flickered again. "Candles!" I shouted.

I sprinted down the hall to the hutch in the kitchen and tried to find a few candles. "Why don't I just buy plain old candles?" I asked as I realized they were all scented. I would never forget the headaches I got from keeping our house lit with all sorts of scented candles during the last big storm, but somehow I had forgotten to buy some that my sinuses could tolerate. Still, I took armfuls of fat and squat candles with multiple wick, cinnamon and apple mostly, and jar candles promising brownies and mocha heaven, and began placing them in every room of the house. I would just need to light them when the power went out. And maybe in the dark I might even eat one if I got desperate.

By the time I took a washcloth to use in bathing Danika, I was exhausted. The lights still flickered, and I shuddered at the thought of going to bed in complete silence while waiting for my husband to come home from the late shift.

"Mommy, did you pray?" Danika asked from the tub.

The question startled me. "What?" I asked.

"Did you pray that we won't lose power?"

It was a simple question but I stuttered like I had no real answer. I knew the answer, though. I hadn't even thought of praying.

"No, baby. I didn't," I admitted.

I watched as my little girl, sitting in the bathtub, bowed her head and lifted her wet hands to her face, the water running down her arms and returning to the tub. I closed my eyes and listened as she prayed to God that we wouldn't lose power.

"In Jesus' name. Amen," she said.

"Amen," I said.

She looked at me and smiled as if it were the easiest thing in the world to do. No rushing around like a crazy woman; no spewing loud commands at a tiny person who was just trying to enjoy her dinner; no rush to somehow stop this this big bad monster of a storm from pounding on our house with fists of wind, invading our home, and threatening to knock down a power line somewhere that led to our house.

Instead there was this calming, soothing trust that was as simple and as natural to Danika as breathing. She trusted her heavenly Father and knew he would take care of us. All we had to do was ask — something I had missed entirely while trying to prepare and fix it all myself.

The water trickled into the tub when I squeezed the washcloth, and Danika giggled as she held her mermaid under the waterfall. She indeed had plenty of time to play since I had hurried her through dinner and her prayer was answered.

We didn't lose power. Not even for a second.

- Joey Rudder

Steps

There are steps

    in our house

        leading to the room

            he must clean.

        "You're not my mother!

            You can't make me clean it."

                "No, I'm not your mother.

                    But I love you as if I were."

                    He's speechless.

                And he cleans his room.

~ *Robin Bayne*

45
Hinin' from de Sunder

The late summer heat was hee-hawing at the tired old air conditioning system in our home, and I was eight months pregnant with our second child…and miserable. We had put Abigail to bed around eight o'clock, and Steve was reading in the den. He had given up his favorite seat, the comfy recliner, where I was stretched out with my swollen feet elevated. All was quiet and I was just beginning to doze when the quiet of the night was shattered.

The storm came up suddenly, angry and ferocious in its attack on our small part of the world. Thunder bombs and lightening explosions made us certain that we were now in a war zone. Time seemed to stand still as the house held its breath waiting on the next flash and subsequent crash. After a while, I began to listen for some sound from my two-year old daughter, but none came.

So even though it was late and my ankles were swollen with pregnancy weight, I told Steve I needed to check on Abigail, upstairs in her bed. I was hoping that she was sleeping through this incredible storm, but I didn't see how.

Her bedroom was at the top of the stairs, and there was a small nightlight in the bathroom across the hall. I paused at her open doorway while my eyes adjusted to the dim light, then I stepped into her room.

Her bed looked empty. My heart quickened with a flutter of fear. Where was she? Where could she be? Just as I was about to call for Steve, my vision grew sharper in the dim light, and I saw her. The long side of the daybed in her tiny bedroom was pushed all the way to the wall, and Abigail face to the wall had pressed her small body firmly against that wall.

I listened for her breathing. She seemed fine, but my heart told me she was awake but had not seen me. I stepped back to the end of her bed and softly called her name.

"Abbe…?" She lifted her chin but didn't turn to look at me.
"Abbe? Are you ok?"
Still she didn't turn, but answered me with words that I will never forget.
"I'm hinin' from de sunder."

Hiding from the thunder. This tiny person had been awakened by the horrible storm, but she didn't cry. She didn't call for help. This tiny person had found a way to handle her fear and get through the storm as best she could.

And that was the moment I knew. Did I love this girl? Immeasurably. Would I always love her? Undoubtedly. But in that moment I knew I was really going to *like* the adult that this person would become. And *liking* is different from loving. Ask any parent of an unruly, smart-mouthed teenager.

It is now twenty years later, and that moment when she was "hinin' from de sunder," when I knew I truly *liked* this person, has proved to be true time and time and time again. I respect her choices. I admire her courage. I am in awe of the talent she displays. I am truly blessed in the way she loves her Momma.

For about ten minutes in her life I thought I had something to do with all this, but then I came to realize I didn't. The Lord just sent her this way.

~ Connie Gatlin

46
The Roses

In my mind, I can still see the pained look that came across her face as I scolded her — my young daughter Marcia, with whom I seemed to be constantly at odds. I had given her money for a school trip and she had spent all of it. I wondered what little trinket she had splurged on this time. But she said nothing and quietly went her way. I was left with my frustration.

Later that day Marcia came and handed me something wrapped in pretty paper. I opened it and found a beautiful spray of wax roses. Then I understood. Instead of spending the money I had given her on something for herself, she had spent it on a gift for me. I could hardly believe it. How ashamed I felt as I remembered the encounter earlier in the day.

I thanked Marcia and put the roses in a vase on the dresser, but every time I looked at them, I felt guilt, shame and sadness. Guilt for being so quick to judge my daughter. Shame that I had reacted in such an unloving way. And sadness because of the hurt I caused her. I just couldn't forgive myself for failing as a mother.

Many times I thought about putting the flowers where I couldn't see them, to save myself those uncomfortable feelings. (Out of sight, out of mind?) But I didn't have the heart to put the roses away somewhere.

It wasn't until years later that I found release from my feelings of guilt, shame, and unforgiveness of myself. All those years I believed God had forgiven me because 1 John 1:9 tells us that God does forgive us our sins if we confess them. I knew that Jesus died on the cross to take away the shame of my sins and failures. I also knew Marcia had forgiven me. Yet, I still couldn't forgive myself. And I couldn't fully accept the forgiveness of God nor my daughter's forgiveness.

Then one day a new thought came to me. *If my daughter has forgiven me and God has forgiven me, what right have I to hold onto my feelings of unforgiveness of myself?*

Now when I look at those roses, I still feel a twinge of regret, but I also think of my daughter's unselfish love. I'm reminded of the peace and joy of forgiveness — God's, my daughter's, and forgiveness of myself. I'm also reminded to not jump to conclusions before I have all the facts.

~ Elsie H. Brunk

47
The Little Red Wheelbarrow

Adele telephoned me. "Hi, Bev," she said. "I wondered if Clint would like to go for a ride with me today in the Thunderbird?"

Clint, our three-year-old son, loved to take rides with Adele. We knew she would take good care of him. He loved to ride with the top down on the convertible and laughed as the wind blew through his hair. They would spend time at the library; have picnics, or anything else Clint loved to do. He'd come home with happy tales of their adventures.

We had recently moved to the southern Oregon coast where we pastored a small church. Adele, a faithful member of our small congregation, had recently purchased a beautiful light blue Ford Thunderbird convertible.

When we had arrived at our pastorate, Adele came to greet us. She told us of her special love for children. She wanted to help in any way she could. With her new car, she looked forward to taking children on rides and having a time of fun. This was a direct answer to prayer, as I had asked the Lord to give Clint friends in this new town, never realizing it would be an adult.

Adele also used her large house to entertain. She loved to have children over to visit. A large fishpond dominated the flower garden and brought delight from the children.

Adele and her husband had retired to this small community. Although he did not attend the church, he always had a kind word to say and loved to entertain anyone she brought to their home.

On this particular day, Adele had something else in mind. She came by and Clint ran to greet her. While he got in the car, she asked me if it would be all right if they were out a little longer than usual. Since it was close to Clint's fourth birthday, I said of course as I felt she was planning a special birthday surprise.

Busy with plans for the coming Sunday, I didn't realize how long they were gone until their return. Clint got out of the car clutching a small red wheelbarrow. He ran up to the porch and said, "Look Mommy, what I got for my birthday from Miss Adele."

"What is it?" I asked.

"It's a red wheelbarrow. I can use it to haul my rocks," Clint said.

"Where did you get it?"

Adele was all smiles. She told Clint they were going to the local toy store to get him a birthday present. She took him to the door of the store and, stopping in the doorway, told him he could buy anything in the store for his birthday present. Clint spent a lot of time looking at all the treasures in the store. Soon his eyes lit up and he said, "That's what I want," referring to the small red wheelbarrow. Since it wasn't a very expensive item, Adele asked him if he was sure he understood he could have anything in the store.

"Oh yes," he replied. "I can haul my rocks around the yard in that. Nippy and I will have lots of fun."

After Clint's birthday, I often sat at our large front window and watched him playing out in the front yard with his dog and the little red wheelbarrow. He would pile rocks in a row and then put them in his wheelbarrow to take to the garden area.

When I think back to that incident, I remember how proud I was of our son and his sweet and gentle spirit. Although he could have picked anything much bigger and more expensive in that toy store, he picked a simple, red plastic wheelbarrow.

What a lesson it was to me, as a young mother, to realize the value of friendship between a child and adult, and to realize how my child taught me the importance of the simple things in life giving such joy.

~ Beverly Hill McKinney

48
First Things

I had a lifetime of firsts planned for you and me
We were going to play tag and skip shells in the sea
We'd build a snowman just to knock him down
I'd teach you to draw and become such a clown

We'd chase butterflies, shoot fireworks, dodge ocean waves
Climb trees, go sledding, get messy with finger paints
I'd teach you to whistle, blow bubbles, rake leaves
Fly kites, ride bikes and great broomstick steeds

I'd teach you to swim and to play hide-and-seek
I'd teach you to pray and to sing and to read
I'd teach you to play ball and be at your first game
Cheering so loudly you might think me insane

I'd drive you to school and help you with classes
Go to church picnics, have hundred yard dashes
There were so many things I thought we would do
We were going to be playmates, me and you

But God took you home even before we could touch
Still I want you to know that I love and miss you so much
So be a good little boy and don't pester the saints
By tugging on robes and tarnishing gates

You know how I've hurt, you've seen me shed tears
Lonely with thoughts of not touching for years
But God is still good; He knows the depths of my pain
He too had a Son but He lost him one day

So I'll draw close to Him and I'll think lots of you
Someday in heaven, First Things we will do
Our roles will reverse and on you I'll depend
To teach me about heaven and places you've been

We'll romp around clouds, walk barefoot on stars
Swim backwards up waterfalls, catch lightning in jars
Drink rocks through a straw and ride bumblebees
Jump in a tall oak and sleep in its leaves

We'll find a bright rainbow to play tug-of-war
This is only a glimpse, there must be so much more
But now we must wait and imagine the day
When at last we're together, and at last son, we play

~ Steve Wilson

49
The Mind of a Child

My son, almost seven, was having a difficult time writing. He was struggling with vision problems and facing surgery. I wanted to help, but not overly protect, him because he needed to learn how to adapt. His assignment was to copy a few sentences and fill in the blank spot with the correct word. He was supposed to do it on his own and he had become upset because I wasn't telling him every letter. He did well if I told him each letter as he wrote, but he needed to move on from that to looking and copying. The goal was for him to accomplish more than he thought he could; but he was getting frustrated. I walked away for a few minutes and when I came back, his five-year-old sister was helping, telling him the letters.

"How long are you going to help me?" he asked her.

"As long as it takes to finish," she answered.

What a great example she was to us!

I helped my children start their own journals when Jessi was four and a half and Russell was six years old. Below are a couple of entries.

> I am six. I learn a lot. I would like to go to a beach. I like to have fun. I like to climb trees and ropes. My favorite food is Jello. I like to wear shorts the most. I want to be a missionary when I grow up. I like Jesus. He never did anything wrong ever. I like my family — Jess, Dad, Mom. I have two dogs — Daisy and Lizzie — and five chickens — Alice, Frank, Speedy, Fluffy and Princess. I gather metal to take to the metal place to get money so I can buy stuff. I like to learn in school with my family. I like math. I like numbers — big ones. I like to learn about planets and moons and solar systems and how far and how many. I like running, kickball, soccer, karate. By Russell

> I am four. I love you. I like ponies and horsies. I like cows. I like to go to the mall. I like to play with my dolls and stuffed animals and penguins if I ever find them. When I grow up I

would like to go to the South Pole. I like bread. I like sparkly clothes. I like music — to sing and I do like dancing and to play the guitar…for real. I do like this — I like all my toys. Jesus is cool. I like him. He is nice. I love my family. I have pets. Daisy is a black dog. Lizzie is a Corgi dog. I have chickens. I like to go to the Y. I like to swim there. I do really like this — I like playing hide and seek. I do really like to go to Chuck E. Cheese. I like to learn about horsies. I pretty much draw good. Everything's doing good. I like running and kickball and karate and soccer. The other thing is that I love everyone. I like riding my bike and ponies. I like long hair. By Jessi

From ages four through seven they had some interesting questions and insights on various subjects:

What are some questions you would like answers to?
  Russell (age 5) What makes volcanoes go? What makes plants grow? Why do we have tractors?
  Jessi (age 4) What makes magnets stick to refrigerators?

How are people like seeds?
  Russell (age 5) We grow, we eat and get water, we run around and work a lot and eat a lot and sweat a lot and do lots of stuff a lot.
  Jessi (age 4) We make us like a little bitty egg and try to grow bigger.

What can we do to grow and nourish ourselves?
  Russell (age 5) Helping God, read scriptures.
  Jessi (age 4) Cook, learn, exercise.

On Prayer
  Russell (age 5) How does he hear everyone when they talk from all the way down here to up in heaven? Does he have a bunch of pipes hooked into all the houses or something?

On batteries
  Russell (age 5) A battery makes things work, it has electric. (How?) It touches one part of metal and then goes to another part of metal and makes it go. (Can you put it in anything and make it work?) No, the

flat part has to go on the spring and the part sticking up has to go on the other end.

Russell (age 5) to Jessi (age 4) on a walk:
Jessi, I forgot my pliers last night and they have rust now. When you grow up and get tools, don't leave them outside at night or they will get rusty.

Why do you think people lived so long at the time of Adam?
Russell (age 5) Because they listened and obeyed the Lord more.

Do you know what f-i-n-e means?
Jessi (age 4) Yes, fine. I'm ok.

Talking about Joshua and Jericho: Is it really possibly that a bunch of loud noise from people can make a city's walls fall down?
Russell (age 6) If God helps, it can happen.

If you could go anywhere in the world for one hour, where would you go?
Russell (age 6) The North Pole…or the South Pole…or Pluto.
Jessi (age 5) Silver Dollar City.

Verbal science review
Where are garter snake eggs hatched?
Jessi (age 5) I don't know. In the garden?

What time of year are snake babies born?
Jessi (age 5) August 10th (her birthday)

How does a sea turtle lay eggs?
Russell (age 7) Dig hole up on sand, lay eggs, cover back. Then go back to the ocean and leave babies by themselves. I would not want to be a sea turtle. I would be left alone.

How does a garter snake feed her young?
Russell (age 7) Ignores them and they have to find their own food even if they get eaten. I would not want to be a baby snake with a mommy like that.

~ Julie A. Hilton

50

The Lesson

While I was driving my son to school, he informed me of a homework assignment that should have been done the previous night. Jeremy is in third grade and hates it, particularly math. If I ask him what he did during the day his answer is, "I don't know."

I would have better luck winning fifty million dollars in a lottery than pulling any sort of school related information out of him. It was a math assignment, of course. When I asked why he didn't tell me about the homework, his response was, "I forgot."

Immediately, I lost my cool and raised my voice, even said harsh words about his irresponsibility.

It seems to be a never ending battle. I actually thought about how many more years he had left in school, looking forward to graduation…if he ever would graduate, that is.

After arriving to work that morning, I had a little discussion with the Lord. "Why does this have to be such a battle?"

I think I did most of the talking in that discussion. My heavenly father, being the patient and caring person he is, let me talk and then he responded.

"My child," he seemed to be saying, "Your child is fearfully and wonderfully made. He may have his quirks and dislikes. He may need more help than other kids. But I made him. I made him for you. He may not fully grasp a math concept, and that frustrates you. However, how have you handled his frustrations? You see, all of my children are imperfect and have idiosyncrasies. Everyone has weak areas. I know your fragile area is patience. What can you learn from today's events? Just because you aren't in school, doesn't mean you can't be taught."

Ouch! That stung.

Now I'd been brought down a couple notches and guilt set in.

Why did I let my son leave the car knowing I was frustrated and angry? I should have hugged him. But I didn't.

My thoughts focused on a passage I'd read before in James 1:19-20 NIV. The verses spoke directly to me. *Be quick to listen, slow to speak and slow to become angry, because human anger does not produce the righteousness that God desires.*

I told God, "I'm sorry."

Although I'm the parent, I know I'm not going to handle every situation ideally. Children forget assignments. They lose jackets and roll eyes. But what matters most is how I react to those situations.

My son is looking to me for guidance. Maybe even to help him learn and like math. He's watching every move, expression and reaction. Children mimic parents. If I want my son to listen, be slow to speak, not be angry, and grow to be righteous, then I need to set the example.

That afternoon, when I picked him up from school, I said what I'd never said to him before. "I'm sorry."

The apology wasn't to excuse his missed homework assignment. It was to teach him what God taught me that day. Jeremy's eyes lit up with relief and he whispered, "Thank you."

Then I did what I wanted to do all day. I hugged him.

With his little arms around me, I felt like I also felt the warm embrace of bigger arms and heard two voices say, "I forgive you."

- Dianna Owens

51
Motherhood: Living the Dream

My first meeting with my son is burned into my memory. It was not after hours of hard labor and nine months of pregnancy. It came after an agonizing four-year wait.

The door opened at our adoption agency and the director walked in with a tiny bundle and handed him to my husband.

My husband unwrapped the blanket and we both just stared at the most beautiful baby boy I had ever seen.

He was perfect. The agonizing years of frustration and wondering if I would ever become a mother melted away in an instant. He was here and he was mine. I thought my heart would burst with happiness.

It no longer mattered when my friends compared their pregnancy and birth stories. I had a baby, too. It didn't matter that he became mine because a young woman had been talked out of having an abortion. It didn't matter that the average one-year wait turned into two years, then three years, and then four years and I could feel myself growing older with each passing day. It just didn't matter anymore. I had a baby.

It seemed his babyhood lasted forever. I savored every moment, committing so much to memory. I was in my element.

Then, out of the blue, when my baby was nearly two years old, our agency called and said they had another baby for us — a little girl.

Ours became a busy life. That sacred time when my son was a baby turned into a time of just keeping my head above water with two little ones, both in diapers. Even though I no longer recorded every moment in my memory bank, I was content and happy and would not trade them for the world.

Life flew by doing all the things that families do. I was too busy living the dream. I never really gave much thought to the time when my children would grow up and leave home. I had friends whose children were leaving home and I chose to not think about it. Basically I was in denial.

When my son was a senior in high school, I was forced to face the fact that my dream was almost over. I had to keep reminding myself that if we, as mothers, do our job correctly, we work ourselves right out of a job because we have raised responsible, independent citizens.

I cried a lot that year in anticipation of his leaving, but I made a conscious choice to see my son as a young adult and not as my baby boy. That helped.

My daughter was home for one more year. There was time to make up for those years when I was too busy to remember all the details of her early childhood. I decided to cherish and document our last year together. Now those experiences are burned in my memory as well, and ready to pour out when she wants to hear about it.

I've resolved that instead of wasting time mourning the fact that my children have grown up and no longer live with me, I celebrate the years we've had living together.

Hey! It's only a matter of time before precious grandchildren will be on the way.

~ *Karen Sawyer*

52
Don't Forget to Pray

An old adage tells us time heals all wounds. I'm not sure about it's healing properties, but we could all use a little more time. Most of us are busy, whether working, taking care of our homes, or volunteering somewhere. For me, as a single mom working one and a half jobs just to keep the lights on and a little gas in the car, life often feels like a three-ring circus. I don't mind the circus so much, but trying to be the ringmaster of all those rings is a bit of a pain.

I had left the office in haste, trying to escape the ever-expanding inbox. I sped home, well aware of dinner that needed to be made, laundry that needed to be done, newsletters that needed to be typed, posters that needed to be created, pieces that needed to be edited, homework that needed to be reviewed, and lunches that needed to be packed, but I supposed I'd survive. After all, I had three hours to accomplish everything before I would collapse out of sheer burnout.

My daughter came wandering slowly to the car when I got to the sitter's. As she piled her backpack, muddy shoes, and herself into the back of the Corolla, I sighed, revved the engine, and said in a frustrated huff, "I'm in a hurry. Come on." I suppose it would have taken too much precious time to say "Hi" before I started grumbling.

"You're always in a hurry," she said.

I felt bad, but I still kept on rushing and huffing and sighing.

By ten that night, I was finally able to get around to prepping my daughter for bed. I knew that hours after she would be snoozing comfortably with her stuffed hippo beneath her fluffy pink quilt, I'd still be up sorting whites and darks, printing final drafts, and making tomorrow's bologna sandwiches. I tucked her in, kissed her hastily on the forehead and offered a very unenthusiastic, exasperated, "Goodnight."

She stopped me in my tracks as I flicked off the Strawberry Shortcake light switch. "Don't forget to pray, Mommy," she commanded.

I was glad she reminded me, but embarrassed that she had to. In my crazy, task-and-worry-filled day, I hadn't left room for the most important thing of all. My daughter had remembered something much more important than laundry and meetings and oil changes and spelling lists.

God tells us often to be still. That takes effort on our part, particularly on busy days. I'm glad my precious daughter reminded me to put prayer to God on my agenda, because he always puts me on his agenda.

~ Autumn Conley

53
The Old Bayonet

I was a young boy the first time my dad explained to me about his old World War II Japanese bayonet. It was hanging on the wall in the basement next to his sawdust-covered jigsaw. It looked like a big knife to me, so I asked him about it.

"That is not a knife, it's a bayonet from the war," he said. "It's Japanese and from Iwo Jima. Right now, it's in a sheath but when you pull it out, it attaches to a rifle. This groove here," he said, pointing to a long groove along the top of the blade, "is the blood groove. That's necessary so it can be pulled out once you stab someone with it. Otherwise you couldn't pull it out." Dad held it out to me. The metal felt cold as I moved my finger along the quarter inch deep blood groove that ran the length of the blade.

Wow! Blood groove and from the war, I thought, even though I did not have a clue what an Iwo Jima was. But I thought it was pretty neat just the same because it was from "the war." I knew Dad had been involved in communications during the war, but until then I had thought that meant he just talked on the telephone.

How come it's not American? I questioned inwardly, but did not ask him. I doubt the importance of pressing my dad for more information ever occurred to my young mind. Now, years later, I can see that such information would have been nothing less than fascinating. I regret not asking him then, as it is now too late to find out why there was no American counterpart hanging on our basement wall.

Many times when playing in our basement, I would play with the old bayonet. It was heavy as I tried to wield it like a sword or thrust it at an imaginary foe. Its small, round spring-loaded catch, located near the end of the handle that locked into place when attached to the front of a rifle, caught my fancy and was fun to push then let snap back into place as it made a clicking sound.

As I grew older, I would take the bayonet down from its resting place and try to imagine it on the end of a rifle and a Japanese soldier crouched in a foxhole, ready for battle. It gave him an extra fifteen and three-quarters inches reach. I knew this because I remember using one of Dad's old tape measures to find out how long the blade was. *"Wow, that's really long,"* I remember thinking. *"He must be invincible."* I wondered then, and now, if the original owner ever had occasion to use his bayonet.

Strange as it may seem, not once during my years living at home did I question why my father would have this wartime keepsake. What events had transpired on that battle-scarred island for it to end up in our basement thousands of miles away?

For the next thirty years or so, I forgot about the bayonet due to college and various jobs in different cities. Then one day it happened — Dad passed away. After the funeral, my nephew, still living in Dad's home state, thought I should have the bayonet and sent it to me. Upon unwrapping it, I noticed a number of changes. The leather holder had long since rotted away. A light layer of rust now replaced the last remnants of paint on the scabbard. The blade had a layer of rust on it and was as dull as ever, maybe more so after all these years.

Determined to learn as much as I could about it, I searched the internet for Japanese bayonets from the WWII era. I learned that it was a Japanese Army Type 30 bayonet, which was first introduced into their military in 1897. Two symbols on the blade identified the arsenal and the subcontractor who manufactured it.

As I run my fingers over the blade, I wonder about its use in the war. Who was the original owner? Did he survive the war? Was he a POW? Did my father find it in one of the infamous caves that were so desperately defended on Iwo Jima?

Alas, there will be no answers. I listen to metal gliding over metal as I slide it back into its worn scabbard and realize that I will have to be content with having Dad's old bayonet in my possession, knowing that it, like him, played a unique part in history.

Holding it in my lap now, I realize just how much this old rusty bayonet means to me because it was a part of my father's younger days — days when he put his life on the line. Maybe I'll never know the answers about the bayonet, but I know about my dad.

When just a child, I didn't realize the impact of what my dad, and others like him, did for me and my freedom.

But I do now.

- Thomas Kienzle

54
What's a Grit?

We had planned to move to the scenic mountains of western North Carolina after Howard's twenty-year retirement from the Federal Prison system. From our point of view our ten-year stay in Illinois was necessary but temporary.

Not so for the children. Although we had tried to condition them to the fact that we would someday move to the mountains, they could not easily face leaving home and life-long friends behind.

Bravely, they tried to accept what was to me good ol' southern living, but to them was all new and foreign. During our first breakfast in a restaurant after moving to the south, one child asked, "Mom, what's a grit?"

"A newspaper," I replied without thinking.

"Yuk!" she exclaimed, while looking over the menu. "Here they eat newspapers for breakfast."

So began our first day in Black Mountain.

Unaccustomed to "roughing it" they bemoaned the fact that our furniture had not arrived (it didn't for three weeks), so we had no television. They weren't the least bit impressed with eating Japanese style.

We did have a phone but no one to call.

They had a phobia about bathing in motels and approved the slogan, "Dirt is Beautiful" and despite the garden growing behind their ears, I was still getting refusals to bathe.

Our hot water heater wasn't hooked up so I borrowed a pot to heat water in. "Maybe I'm dirty," David admitted skeptically, "but you aren't about to get me into that pot!"

With four children against two adults, the battle of Illinois vs. North Carolina raged.

"But look at the lovely view of the mountains," I implored. "You don't get that in Illinois." They had to admit I was right about that.

We all know a mother can't win that easily.

The following morning they awoke me with, "Somebody had a lot faith last night!"

"What are you talking about?" I asked sleepily.

"Somebody moved your mountains," they replied smugly.

I moaned and rolled over.

"Really! Go look."

To appease them, I went and looked. The shock was unbearable. Without my mountains, I had no recourse but to acclaim the praises of Illinois.

Slowly it dawned.

"That's fog," I breathed, relieved. "It will lift."

"We still don't have anything to do!" they wailed.

Responsibility, I decided, was what they needed. Each child was assigned one day a week to wash the dishes. The first three days went fine.

The fourth day, my four-year-old. awakened me with moans of, "Mommy, I'm starving."

"It's not daylight,"I murmured. "You can't be hungry."

"But I am. Fix me an egg with a bump on it and make everybody get up and eat."

Oh, no! I realized. It's her day to wash the dishes!

After breakfast, Howard took the children out to trim, cut limbs and clean debris from the yard while I waded through the kitchen and was reminded of the adage, "If a child wants to wash the dishes, she's not old enough."

The children raced in, yelling for me to come and look.

Rushing outside, I was positive something they heard growl in the woods must be eating Howard.

"A snake! A snake!" they screamed in unison, as the black creature slithered into his hole, then stuck his head out, eyeing us suspiciously.

I managed a feeble smile, and returned to the house with a sinking feeling, knowing a house without a happy family is not a home. I seriously wondering about the move we had made. All the obstacles...now snakes.

Later the children got out pencils and paper and began writing to their friends in Illinois, excitingly discussing and writing about their "pet snake," not in Mom and Dad's backyard...but in "our" backyard.

"Our!"

A day later only added to their delight. A snakeskin was discovered near the front porch. They watched as a snake slithered into his hole under the front porch near the front door, then vividly described to me the markings on the two-foot long body.

Their snake! Their friends in Illinois had only ordinary, common, everyday cats and dogs!

I didn't know what kind of snake it was, and was doubtful I would ever find out because there simply wasn't room for the two us of near that front porch.

But children loved him and began accepting Black Mountain as home, grits snakes and all.

I, on the other hand, was having nightmares about snakes.

~ *Yvonne Lehman*

55
Katelyn's Cross

Instead of bouncing, running, or skipping as was her usual style, six-year-old Katelyn walked into the house after returning home from church. Her small head was lowered and her forehead furrowed.

"What's wrong, Katelyn?" I asked.

She looked up at me, but the frown remained.

"My teacher told me something sad. Let me get a piece of paper and I'll show you."

She placed a white sheet of paper and a box of markers on the coffee table, got down on her knees, and went to work. I squinted, confused as I watched Katelyn pull a brown marker from the box.

"Don't watch, Nana. I'll show you when I'm finished."

"Okay," I said, and went into the kitchen to prepare lunch. In just a few minutes, Katelyn walked into the kitchen.

"Here, Nana. This is what's wrong." She handed me her drawing. Katelyn had drawn a yellow sun in one corner, grass sprouted from the bottom of the page, and a big brown cross reached to the sky. Scrawled in childish handwriting were these words: "Jesus died here. So sad."

I looked at Katelyn and our eyes met. "He died, Nana," she said. "Jesus died on the cross, and I am sad. Does that make you sad, too?" I heard sadness she tried to choke back. My precious granddaughter had learned what Jesus endured to be our Savior, and the awful truth broke her sweet heart.

"Oh Katelyn, yes, it makes me sad, but I need to tell you the rest of the story. Jesus died on the cross because he loves us so much. He died on the cross for you and for me and for everyone in the world so that we can be forgiven when we sin, or do something bad. Jesus died so that someday we can go to heaven and live forever with all the people we love. And do you want to know the best part of the story, Katelyn? Jesus came back to life — did you know that? God raised Him from the dead and took him to heaven where he still lives today. We can talk to Him anytime we want by praying."

"Oh," she said and I watched the sorrow melt from her face. "That's good, Nana. Okay, I'm going to play."

Katelyn heard the news, and joy returned to her heart. She bounced down the hallway to her room, all the while singing, "Jesus loves me, this I know."

Katelyn's reaction to hearing that Jesus died on the cross caused my heart to ache, and I experienced anew the sorrow of my Savior's torturous death. But then I remembered the rest of the story, and joy flooded my soul.

Thank you, Jesus — for the rest of the story.

~ Susan Dollyhigh

56
My Huckleberry Friend

When my five-year-old grandson, Owen, arrived on a warm September morning, he bounded up the stairs and grinned, ready for action! Since Owen loves "huckles," as he calls huckleberries, we headed outdoors to pick some for tarts.

After picking only a handful, Owen declared, "I think that's enough." Off he ran to check the apple trees for fruit while I kept picking berries. Fortunately, I had already picked several cupfuls before he came.

Soon he reported, "No apples," then surveyed my berry stash before helping me pick a few more. After we had enough, we went inside to wash and sugar the huckles.

"Yum-m-m," he said as he sampled the sweet but tart berries. I simmered the berries gently for a few minutes, and then Owen and I sat down at the kitchen table to make tart shells. "Chick-a-dee-dee, chick-a-dee-dee," Owen repeated as he mimicked the bird chirping outside the window.

I was so focused on baking, I hadn't even heard the bird's song until Owen echoed it. "What kind of bird is that?" I asked him. "Is it a chickadee?"

With his hands deep in the bowl mixing flour and butter, he continued, "Chick-a-dee-dee, chick-a-dee-dee," smiling as the words rolled off his tongue. Once the dough was mixed, we rolled out the crust for tart shells. With all the flour he got on his apron, I considered baking it too.

While the tart shells baked, we whipped the cream. Of course, Owen licked off the remaining sweet cream from the beaters. When everything was ready, we filled some tart shells with berries and topped them with whipped cream, eager to sample our tasty treat.

Owen ate a tart, then licked his fingers and gave me an approving blue-huckleberry smile.

I packaged the remaining tart shells, huckleberry sauce, and whipped cream for Owen to take home and share with his family.

Before Owen came, I had debated whether I had time for him that day.

After all, I needed to practice my talk on "FANtastic Grandparenting." Later, I realized spending time with him was the perfect preparation. After all, there's nothing like the lessons a five-year-old can teach.

I learned:
1. Listen for the birds, and enjoy their songs.
2. Put your all into life, even if you get flour on your apron.
3. Savor every lick of whipped cream.
4. Take time for the little (and big) people in your life.

I'm glad I took time for Owen — because kindergartners don't keep. Now, I'm looking forward to more precious moments with my huckleberry friend.

Owen's Huckleberry Tarts

You don't need to be the Queen of Hearts to bake tarts.
You can substitute blueberries if wild "huckles" aren't available.

Crust for Tart Shells

Ingredients:
1 cup all-purpose flour
1 teaspoon sugar
¼ teaspoon salt
⅓ cup butter or shortening
2 to 3 tablespoons cold water

Directions:
1. Combine dry ingredients.
2. Cut in shortening or butter.
3. Add water to moisten.
4. Mix well, and roll ⅛-inch thick on floured cutting board.
5. With a 3-inch cookie cutter, cut 12 circles from the dough.
6. Place circles in mini muffin tins to make tart shells. Prick sides and bottoms 3 or 4 times to prevent puffing.
7. Bake at 450º for 5 to 9 minutes until lightly browned. Cool in muffin tin.

Fresh Huckleberry Filling

Ingredients:
- ½ cup granulated sugar
- 1 tablespoon cornstarch
- 1 tablespoon water
- 1 teaspoon lemon juice.
- 1 cup whole fresh huckleberries
- ⅓ cup mashed fresh huckleberries
- Whipped cream for topping

Directions:
1. In a 1-quart saucepan combine sugar and cornstarch.
2. Stir in water and lemon juice.
3. Add mashed ⅓ cup berries.
4. Bring to boil; reduce heat and simmer a few minutes to thicken. Remove from heat.
5. When sauce is cool, gently stir in 1 cup fresh berries. Refrigerate until ready to serve.
6. Spoon huckleberry filling into tart shells. Top with whipped cream.

Optional: Garnish with a sprig of mint and a few berries

~ Lydia E. Harris

57
Cow Creamer

Mother and I slipped into our flowered Sunday dresses. She tied a red ribbon into a lock of my straw-colored hair. I even wore sandals that my next older sister had outgrown. I had awakened early that morning, excited to go with mother to Tarhala farm for a visit.

Tarhala was was a substantial country home near Eurajoki in western Finland. My mother and my older siblings had lived there during the war years, while father fought in the war, and while we were homeless refugees.

My parents were originally from Karelian isthmus, located in southeastern Finland, which was lost in war and ceded to Russia. My family had to flee and leave their beloved ancestral home behind. Almost a half a million Karelians became refugees just like my family.

I was so glad that I was born after the war on the resettlement farm and in the house that father built. I only knew Eurajoki and loved our home.

Mother and I walked out of our farmyard to the dirt road toward the village. We passed father's fields where golden wheat swayed in the early morning breeze. As we walked over the weathered wooden bridge a pair of geese waddled toward us and greeted us with friendly honks.

We passed by a butter-colored farmhouse in need of paint, lush meadows with cows, and then we cut through a parcel of forest that had burned down. Pink fire-weed flowers bloomed among the charred tree stumps. The air smelled smoky and earthy. A cuckoo in the distance sang a complaint over the lost trees.

I followed mother, scampering to keep up with her pace. We walked in silence, at times holding hands. I was getting very tired, and just then we arrived at Tarhala. A chained dog stood aloof and was aroused to barking, announcing our arrival. I was glad it was not running free.

Mother reminded me of good manners as she knocked on the door. I took off my sandals and mother gave me socks to put on as was our Finnish custom. The door opened. I was whisked in the sunny *tupa* (family room type of kitchen). Mother and her friend went to the enclosed back porch to talk.

On the table in front of me a house maid placed a tray which held a cow-shaped creamer filled with milk, a delicate coffee cup with matching saucer, and a plate with a slice of *pulla* (sweet yeast bread).

A small marmalade cat ambled toward my chair and rubbed my legs. It jumped on my lap. Startled, I pushed it back down. The cat didn't interest me.

I could not take my eyes off the cow creamer. It was the prettiest thing that I had ever seen. The cow was shiny, mostly white with several honey-colored spots on her body. She had dark friendly eyes and wore a gilded bell around her neck. Frothy, warm fresh milk poured out of her pink mouth when I lifted her by her tail-handle.

Mesmerized, I tilted that sacred cow and poured her heavenly milk into my cup. I wanted to take her home!

"I must have this cow, I need this cow, I should have this cow, I deserve this cow!" I chanted mutely over and over again during the hour-long visit. I argued with myself whether or not to kidnap the cow creamer, but I was already six years old and knew that stealing was wrong and that I would feel guilty and not enjoy my stolen cow anyway.

It would also make mother sad and I didn't want to add troubles to her hard life. In addition to her home, she had lost two children to sicknesses and two more during the misery of the war times.

No, even though I had but a few play-things at home, it would not excuse the theft of the beautiful cow creamer. Also our hostess would easily guess who took it, since I seemed to be the only child present.

I knew God saw right through me into my heart. I sighed sorrowfully but left the cow creamer there.

On the long way home, I lagged behind Mother, deep in thought but with untroubled conscience.

Years later, my daughter Sara, who knew about my temptation to steal the beautiful cow creamer, saw a similar one in a shop and bought it for me.

"Mama," she said, "now you finally have your own cow creamer."

I felt a kinship with the psalmist who wrote in Psalm 119:29-30 NIV: *Keep me from deceitful ways; be gracious to me and teach me your law. I have chosen the way of faithfulness; I have set my heart on your laws.*

Over the years my sons, too, have brought home cow creamers. So today I am a content keeper of an entire herd of gifted porcelain cows.

What a blessing!

~ Mirijam Budarz

58

Grandchild Journal, a Legacy of Love

What can I leave my grandchildren?

I heard other grandmothers discussing the quilts they were making for their grandchildren. But when I tried quilting, I put in five stitches and took out three. Right then I decided it wasn't for me. I'm not a quilter. But I still thought it would be wonderful to be able to give each of my grandchildren a quilt I'd made.

One day when I was inwardly lamenting that my grandchildren would never be blessed with quilts from my hands, this thought came: *The journals I'm keeping for my grandchildren could be my quilts to them.*

I started a journal for each of our twelve grandchildren at the time they were born. Following are parts of the first entry in our oldest grandchild's journal:

> Dear Jason, our first grandchild,
> We love you! Welcome to this great big world! As I write, you are exactly one day old. Last night at this time (10:55 p.m.) you came into the world and were eagerly welcomed by your mommy and daddy. They (and all of us) had waited those long nine months, wondering just who you would be. Your mommy and daddy loved you so much, even before you were born...

I then wrote how excited all of us were, that we were happy he was born safely, and about my special privilege of holding him when he was only twelve hours old.

I kept Jason and his brother, Clinton, while their parents worked, so I had plenty to write about in their earlier years. After their family moved to another part of our state I now make entries in their journals after we've had contact by phone or through visits. I do the same for our three Pennsylvania grandchildren.

A journal is a good way to share our faith with our grandchildren. When Nathan and his sisters, Katie and Madison, were dedicated in a Sunday morning service, my husband and I traveled to Pennsylvania to attend. Along with other comments, I included the following in each of their journals:

> Grandpa and I were glad we could take part in your dedication. We promised to do whatever we can to help you grow up to serve God. We pray that you will always love God and serve Him with all your heart, soul, mind, and strength. That is the only way to have true peace and joy.

One important message I try to convey often in my grandchild journals is how much I (and Grandpa) love them. I remind them too, that they are special persons whom God created and loves dearly. I also recount the happenings in their lives, their growth and development, and the cute things they say and do. In Clinton's journal I wrote about his saying he doesn't like the kind of kiwi with "fur on." Our grandson, Caamon, lives close by. I wrote this entry in his journal when he was almost two:

> You did some really cute things today, Caamon. When I took you along upstairs, you sat down and talked to yourself in the full-length mirror. You kept saying, "Whatcha' doin'?" Then you'd answer, "Playin' trucks." When I told you we had to go to another room, you looked in the mirror and said, "Be right back!" You're saying many five-word sentences now. Such a boy!

When Caamon, his three brothers, Jessie, Victor, and Trace, and their sister, Anna Faith, come to visit, I have entries to make in all their journals.

I felt blessed to witness the birth of Grandaughter Elyssa in Oregon. Three years later, I helped care for her new brother, Johnny. Phone calls, emails, and yearly visits now provide material for their journals.

I write about our grandchildren's feelings and hard experiences, hoping this may be useful in helping them understand themselves better as adults. When they have a problem, I write of my concern, but I also try to include encouragement and hope.

In addition to books made for journaling, hardcover record books work well. Spiral notebooks may offer greater flexibility, but bound books are more durable and less likely to have pages torn out. Sometimes I include a clipping, a drawing by the grandchild, or their picture inserted between the pages.

There are times when I can't write in a grandchild's journal right after an event, so in the back of my own journal, I keep a sheet of paper for each grandchild, with his or her name at the top. When I write about them in my journal, I put the date on their sheet. Later I can refer to those dates and recapture the happenings as I write them in their journals.

I pray that someday my grandchildren's journals will be a special blessing to them, not only in understanding themselves better, but also to reassure them of their specialness and God's love for them in those times when they may be tempted to doubt their self-worth and struggle with low self-esteem, or have feelings of not being lovely or loved.

Keeping journals requires a lot of time and work. But then, so does quilting. And while quilts are usually a labor of love by grandmothers, either grandparent can keep journals. In some families, Grandpa may be the one who enjoys writing more than Grandma does. Or perhaps both could share in writing grandchild journals.

The fact that I'm not a quilter no longer bothers me. I believe that our grandchildren will feel my (and their grandpa's) warmth and deep love for them when they read their journals, just as they would feel the warmth of a quilt and the love that went into its making.

In fact, that happened when I gave their journals to our four oldest grandchildren. Their comments…and tears, in the case of our granddaughter (as reported by her parents) told me their journals were just as meaningful to them as a quilt would have been.

I consider those grandchild journals my legacy of love.

Suggestions for Making a Grandchild Journal

1. Choose a durable book for the journal.

2. Start when — or even before — the grandchild is born. Begin *now*, even if the grandchild is already older. If keeping a journal seems too difficult, write in letter form and make it ongoing.

3. Always be positive in your writing. Never criticize or discourage the grandchild or write negatively about another person. If there are hard situations in your grandchild's life, write about those in a way that will be encouraging and helpful to them.

4. If you can't make an entry right away and don't keep a journal of your own, jot notes on a paper or calendar, so you can later record facts and details accurately.

5. Consider your time and effort an important investment in your grandchild's future.

6. Pray that the journal will enhance the life of your grandchild when she or he is older, and that it will be a means of drawing them closer to the Lord.

~ *Elsie H. Brunk*

59

Cat Funerals

Jewel was a favorite cat. The last time seen she was dead on the living room floor. When four-year-old Nicholas was asked by his sister if he'd seen the cat dead on the floor he replied, "No, the last time I saw her she was on the table."

Nick's sister planned the funeral. She scoured the back yard to find the finest rock to be painted for a headstone. Of course, there would be a service. Prayers needed to be said so Jewel could get into cat heaven since Jewel had never been saved or baptized.

That was all a little fuzzy since it might be different for cats. How they got in. Maybe St. Peter kept a different book for animals and maybe there was a different way to get into heaven since cats hated anything to do with water whether it be a sprinkle, a dunk, or a pouring. They preferred dry washing and taking chances on hairballs, which were much more likely than meteor collisions. So maybe that was penance enough.

However, Jewel's exploits would be remembered, at least for one day anyway.

When Nick showed up for the funeral and saw the tombstone, he pitched a hissy fit. It sat at the head of the freshly dug mound of dirt with the name Jewel painted on in big bold letters.

"What's the problem with the tombstone?" asked Nick's sister. "Jewel deserved to have something nice written about her. She was a good mouser!"

"It's my very favorite rock," wailed Nick. "And you've taken it and painted stuff all over it."

Nick screamed, cried and vehemently protested. The year before at another cat funeral, Nick had also been disruptive. He'd come out during the service asking for puddin'.

His sister had said, "We're not messing with you and your puddin'. We're trying to have a cat funeral. Go away."

Nick ran into the house and found a container of puddin' and ran back outside. Without a spoon.

"You can't eat puddin' without a spoon," said his sister. So, Nick ran back inside, and later returned with a spoon. No one knew where he'd found the spoon or if the spoon was clean or if the spoon was dirty. But Nick ate puddin' during the eulogy.

And now, Nick screamed, wailed and kicked out his frustration because Sister had found his special favorite rock in all the world and had desecrated it, all because of a cat.

Sister couldn't wait to call Great-Grandmother to tell her all about the latest cat funeral and how they'd eulogized Jewel. Great-Grandmother called Great-Aunt and told her she needed to get the family together and drive up from Florida to attend the next cat funeral.

Great-Aunt said, "I'm not driving all the way up to Tennessee to attend a cat funeral."

Great-Grandmother said, "Well, you might think about it, they serve puddin'."

Great-Aunt said, "Well, in that case, I might have to change my mind."

~ Vicki Moss

60

I Dreamed a Dream

I sat for over two-and-a-half hours, completely enthralled. The raw emotion evoked through their voices mesmerized me. I was only eight years old, but I began to dream that one day I would be a participant in the captivating story and music of *Les Miserables*.

The Tenth Anniversary Concert filmed at London's Royal Albert Hall became a daily staple in my life. When not watching the film, I listened to the cassette tapes over and over. By ten I was able to sing every part in every song. I dreamed of singing a part on Broadway.

In college I yearned for a small role in a community organization. I figured that the role of Fantine — by far the most difficult female part of the program — would forever be out of my reach.

After college, with my deep love for music, I joined a small community choir. In the fall of 2014, our director announced that we would be singing Broadway numbers. My heart nearly stopped when she presented the music of *Les Miserables*. It was a choral arrangement that covered the highlights of the score, which included solo numbers. Auditions were held and I hoped for one of the small solos.

During auditions my knees shook and my voice was unsteady. After I finished I sat in the hall listening to the other auditions, certain that I would not get a part. There were too few numbers and many talented vocalists.

That night I realized that sometimes dreams don't come true. I knew that the words of acceptance might not happen for me.

So, when I got a call a week later, I was surprised to hear my director's voice. She said, "Cara, I think you're perfect for the role of Fantine in 'I Dreamed a Dream.' If you like it, the part is yours."

I was overwhelmed by the immensity of what she was offering. I accepted with breathless excitement, humbled by her faith in me.

"I Dreamed a Dream" was not something I deserved — I was no more worthy than any other member. But something prompted our director to take a chance on me. Under the stage lights on opening night a childhood dream of over two decades was realized.

If we're willing to work for them, and to exercise patience in their arrival, then who says we won't hear the words that make our dreams come true?

~ Carole Anne Pearson

61

All Shook Up

Elvis Pressley, king of Rock 'n Roll, sang a song titled, "All shook up."
I remember the day my world became "shook up." We were living in Southern Illinois when it happened.

I'd recently given birth to my fourth child, Cindy. She was asleep in her bassinet beside the couch in the living room. Three-year old David was playing in the front yard. Five-year-old Lisa and seven-year-old Lori were playing across the street at a friend's house..

A neighbor was working in the yard. My husband had gone to the store for some needed items and would return from the local store in a few minutes.

It was a warm, sunny Saturday morning in September, during a time when you could turn your back on a child for a few minutes without worrying about their safety — particularly in our suburban neighborhood where most of the residents had young children and a few older people looked out for them as if they were their own beloved grandchildren.

Without a concern about my girls across the street, my son in the yard, and my baby in the living room, I went into the kitchen to wash dishes. Peace and joy filled my heart as I looked out at the sunshine on our back yard where we had a family pet, a beagle hound named Snoopy, a swing set, and a backyard fence. Beyond the yard lay an open field where neighborhood children often gathered to play tag, ball, or climb the big old maple tree. Neighbors' homes flanked the field.

Suddenly, my hands began to tremble. The dish in my hands slipped back into the rippling water in the sink. My knees felt like they'd buckle and my feet felt unsteady on the floor. What was happening to me? I'd felt strong enough to leave the hospital on the second day after giving birth to Cindy. Had I come home too soon? I was almost over the hill at age thirty-two — getting to be middle-aged. Was I fainting?

I began to make my way to the living room when I heard the dishes rattling in the kitchen cabinets. My hand grasped the door casing as I reached the living room. No, I knew I was not strong enough to shake an entire house. What was happening? My world began to shake, rumble, and threaten to fall apart.

Was it the end of the world? Would Gabriel's trumpet blast any minute? Or would the ground open up and swallow us all? This was tornado alley, but I neither felt nor saw the effects of any wind. Then I realized, although I'd never been in one before, this was an earthquake.

Feeling like I was walking on a floor of Jello, I finally reached the front door. I looked back at my baby, sleeping soundly, rocking in her straight-legged bassinet. I looked out at my son, crawling on the ground, trying to get to me. What should I do? Yank up my sleeping baby and run from the house? Leave her there for the house to fall in on her? Run into the yard and bring my son inside? I opened the screen door, and held onto the trembling door casing while my knees threatened to give way.

"Come on, honey. You can do it. Come on," I urged David, now on all fours trying to crawl to me. He couldn't make any progress. It looked as if he were trying to be steady on a sea of sinking sand. The grass slipped from his grasping fingers. He couldn't get hold of anything to steady him. He couldn't walk. He couldn't crawl. He could only look at his mommy with big eyes that seemed to say, "Do something. Help me."

I couldn't help. I too, was helpless as my newborn baby and my three-year-old son. I stood in the doorway, literally shaking in my shoes, with my heart thundering against my chest.

Then it stopped. My world stopped shaking. My son rose to his feet and hurried inside where I folded him in my arms, assuring him everything was all right. It was just a little earthquake, and no, it probably would never happen again.

Soon, the neighbors came out of their houses and we all shakily told of our own experiences of lamps toppling over, books and jars falling from shelves and crashing to the floor.

I realized that day that life is not so stable.

My sweet girls, whom I thought were inside playing, were instead outside coloring on a neighbor's fuel-oil tank. They learned a lot about soap and water that day and how hard it is to scrub waxy crayon off a fuel-oil tank.

"Lord," I prayed. "My world is shaky. I am shaky even though the earth seems stable again. But I don't want to be as oblivious to the dangers as my newborn, sleeping peacefully in her bassinet while the world around her seems to be falling apart.

"I need to know that my sweet girls aren't always peacefully playing in someone's house. Sometimes they're out coloring someone's fuel-oil tank.

"How can I have a solid foundation in an insecure world?"

I thought, *I'll keep my hand in yours, Lord. Only you can keep me steady. I have lives to build. Somewhere I read that the pyramids were not built on sand. They had to get down to bare rock. I have four little pyramids to build. I want the foundation to be strong and structure point to you.*

Then, my own foundation must be built on the solid rock, Lord, and I must keep my eyes on you. My own earthly wisdom is insecure.

I thought of the time Lori was looking at a picture of Jesus knocking on a door. To her question, "Why is he knocking?" I answered, "It symbolizes his knocking on our heart's door."

"Oh," she said in amazement, "that's why we hear that thump-thump-thump."

Hmmm. Maybe when we hear the thump-thump-thump of uncertainty and fear, we can just remember that Jesus is knocking, and open the door. He will be our security.

Like the words of a song, "My faith is built on nothing less, than Jesus' blood and righteousness. On Christ, the solid rock, I stand. All other ground is sinking sand."

When I'm "all shook up," I need a lot more than the king of Rock 'n Roll. I need the King of kings, the one who holds the world in his hands.

~ *Yvonne Lehman*

62

You Are Beautiful!

Our week-long vacation included three fun filled mornings at two different waterparks. As many other six-year-old boys, our son had battle scars to bear witness to his conquering the body slides, inner tube rides, zip lines, and climbing many rock steps — while barefoot.

As I looked at him sitting in the back seat I saw an almost-healed scrape on the top of his left foot, dried blood on the top of his right foot and toes, red abrasions on both inner thighs, various small bruises on his arms, and a well healed scar on his upper lip from a surgery when he was a baby.

Interestingly enough, as I looked at him with all his wounds I said to my husband, "He is the most beautiful thing I've ever seen."

There is a truth that some may never have heard, or if we have, we can't quite believe it. The truth is this: God sees us as I saw my son — beautiful.

Yes, he sees our sin, our hidden secrets and our shame. He sees our scars from hurts long ago or the bloodied wound that we just received. He hurts when our wounds are re-opened and the pain seems unbearable. He sees us, bloodied and battle weary, yet, he doesn't turn away because we aren't perfect. No, He looks at us, as his children, through eyes filled with love and says, "You are beautiful!"

Close your eyes and let those words seep into your soul. The God of the universe, the creator, thinks you are beautiful.

~ *Cindy Wilson*

We worry what a child will become tomorrow,
yet we forget that he is someone today.

~ *Stacia Tauscher*

Children need love, especially when they don't deserve it.

~ *Harold Hulbert*

"Let the children come to me. Don't stop them! For the Kingdom of God belongs to such as these."

~ Jesus (Mark 10:15 NLT)

About the Authors

Carolyn Barnum moved from Jackson, Michigan to Wesley Village Retirement Community in Wilmore, Kentucky in 2012. She and her husband, Clair Barnum, were married for 59 years before his death in 2009. They traveled extensively in the United States, England, Scotland, Wales, Italy, Switzerland and Austria. During her career she held various secretarial and executive assistant positions. She coordinates Write People, a writer's group in Wesley Village. She enjoys writing, reading, involvement in various activities at Wesley Village, and spending time with friends.

Robin Bayne is an award-winning author of 17 novels, novellas and short stories. She compiled a collection of devotionals for writers titled *Words To Write By*. She lives in Maryland with her husband of 25 years. Visit her at www.robinbayne.com

Shirley G. Brosius is the author of *Sisterhood of Faith: 365 Life-Changing Stories About Women Who Made a Difference*, a daily devotional book featuring historic and contemporary Christian women with messages from their lives. She enjoys writing, speaking and keeping up with her husband, two sons, daughters-in-laws and five grandchildren. She also co-authored *Turning Guilt Trips into Joy Rides* along with two women with whom she shares a speaking ministry as Friends of the Heart.

Elsie H. Brunk and her husband of 56 years have four children, 12 grandchildren, and four great-grandchildren. Her devotionals and articles have been published in *Christian Parenting Today, Live, The Family Digest, Standard, The Secret Place,* and other periodicals. Her book, *Encouragement in the Wilderness — Devotionals for Days of Discouragement, Depression, and Despair* was published in 2002. In 2011, this book was published by Lighthouse Publishing of the Carolinas as an e-book titled, *Streams of Living Water for a Thirsty Soul*. Visit Elsie on her website: elsiehbrunk.com or contact her at ebrunk@rica.net.

Rob Buck is a business owner who ministers to men in the work place. He is husband to Betsy, his bride of 33 years, is father of four and grandfather of four, with one more on the way. He attends Columbia Crossroads Church in Columbia South Carolina and co-leads a Home Fellowship Group. Rob is president of Alpha Training and Services, an IT training company and treasurer of Focused Living, www.focusedliving.com. Rob enjoys gardening, chicken farming, pool and cycling. He also plays disc golf and has built an 18-hole course on his property. Rob is a member of Word Weavers International. He has written for a number of magazines and newspapers including the *Christian Standard, Columbia Star* and *Reach Out Columbia*. Rob's first novel, *Beyond Time*, was published by OakTara in 2007 and the sequel, *Home Remains*, is in the publishing process. He is currently working on a devotional, *Joy in the Journey*.

Mirjam Budarz lives in beautiful coastal Wilmington, North Carolina. She and her husband have four children, two daughters-in-law, one son-in-law, four grandchildren, two dogs, two cats and foster-care horses. She loves to write and brag about God, His goodness, deeds and word. She feels called to pray and to bless people. She has lived in Finland, Germany and the USA and sounds foreign wherever she goes. She went to nursing school in Germany and worked as a geriatric nurse while there. She is a member of Wilmington Word Weavers and blogs occasionally at their site. She has been journaling almost half a century, some of her many writings have been published, one about gardening "Sharing Beauty" by local newspaper, and one about a simple prayer "French Tutor Needed" in the Guidepost book, *Extraordinary Answers to Prayer, Unexpected Answers*. She also has done illustrations for two children's books. She writes nonfiction and fiction. You can contact at mirjam.budarz.com or mirjambudarz@yahoo.com.

Joann M. Claypoole is the author of *DoveStories,* a children's chapter book series (ages 5-9) and *The Gardener's Helpers*. She's recently written a children's picture book, *Coo Says You Are Loved* (ages 2-5), and has several stories featured in three books in *Divine Moments, Christmas Moments,* and *Spoken Moments* (Grace). Joann co-wrote the Television documentary script, *My Last Hope,* for National House of Hope hosted by Candace Cameron Bure (2011). She writes songs, plays, articles, and blogs at joannclaypoole.wordpress.com. She's a member of SCBWI and Word Weavers. Joann serves local and international missions and sings on the praise and worship leading team at her local church. She is a wife, mother of four sons, has three grand babies, two crazy canines, and owns a salon/spa in sunny central Florida.

Autumn Conley spent many years working in various offices but escaped Cubicle Land in 2009 to become a full-time freelance book editor. She enjoys spending time with her daughter, Cissy, her family, and her three dogs. Writing has been a lifelong passion for Autumn, and she began her writing career at the age of fourteen. Over the years, she has penned many essays, short stories, poems, and articles and has been published in anthologies, such as *Chicken Soup, Soul Matters for Mothers, The Bad Hair Day Book,* and in magazines including *Home Life, All You* and *New Moon for Girls*. Her children's story, "Where Does the Snow Go?" was recently accepted for publication in *Primary Treasures*. In 2005, she self-published two books, a suspense novella and a Christian teen novel, and she is currently at work on a new novel. In addition to writing and editing, Autumn busies herself with geocaching, a hobby that helps her enjoy the great outdoors with family and friends.

Tracy Crump has written numerous articles and devotionals for publications such as *Focus on the Family, ParentLife, Mature Living,* and *Quiet Hour,* and she is a columnist for *Southern Writers Magazine*. Storytelling is her passion, as evidenced by her many stories that appear in *Chicken Soup for the Soul* and other anthologies. As co-director of Write Life Workshops, Tracy conducts workshops and webinars which encourage others to "Write Better, Write Now!" Her love of teaching also takes her to conferences where she helps writers hone their craft. But her most important job is Grandma to little Nellie. Visit Tracy at WriteLifeWorkshops.com or TracyCrump.com and subscribe to her free e-newsletter, *The Write Life,* which includes story callouts.

Emily Marett Disco is a former award-winning swimmer. She is married to Andy Disco (a swimmer), who plans to become a veterinarian technician. Emily wrote her poem when in fifth grade and is now a student at the University of North Carolina at Asheville, majoring in religious studies with a minor in psychology. She and Andy have three cats: Bagheera, Samba, and Sebastian. A recent addition to their family is Lucy, a delightful energetic Yorkshire Terrier.

Greg M. Dodd is the author of the Christian novel, *A Seed for the Harvest*, winner of the 2015 Independent Publishers' Illumination Awards Enduring Light Silver Medal for Christian Fiction. Greg lives in Columbia, South Carolina with his wife, Caroline, and their Anatolian Shepherd, Desmond. He earned his bachelor's and master's degrees from the University of South Carolina and works as an IT professional for an energy-based holding company. Greg is active in his church home, Shandon Baptist, teaching evangelism training and a Sunday school class for young adults. He is currently writing *The Last Harvest*, a sequel to *A Seed for the Harvest*. For more information, visit gregmdodd.com.

Susan Shelton Dollyhigh is a freelance writer and speaker. She is a contributing author in *Spirit and Heart: A Devotional Journey*, *Faith and Finances: In God We Trust*, *The Ultimate Christian Living*, *God Still Meets Needs*, *Divine Moments*, and *Christmas Moments*. A version of "Daddy Talked?" was published in *I Believe in Heaven* with Cecil Murphey and Twila Belk. Susan's articles have appeared in *Connection Magazine*, *Exemplify Magazine*, *Mustard Seed Ministry*, *P31 Woman*, *The Upper Room* and *The Secret Place*.

Susan Engebrecht has written for a variety of magazines, *Chicken Soup for the Soul* books, Lighthouse Publishing of the Carolinas, and worked as a columnist. She has won a number of writing and speaking awards, judges writing and speaking contests, served on the board for Wisconsin Writers Association and is currently co-director for the Green Lake Christian Writers Conference held each year in August. Her husband, aka in her writings as Knight-in-faded-blue-jeans, a bossy puggle, and five take-your-breath-away-brilliant grandchildren provide endless joy and writing material.

Sandra Fischer taught high school English and owned a Christian bookstore in Indiana for several years before retiring and devoting time to writing. Many of her stories and articles are gleaned from her experiences growing up in the Midwest. She has been published in *Guideposts*, various anthologies, in *Faithwriters Magazine* online and on the Faithwriters website: www.faithwriters.com. Sandra lives in South Carolina with her husband, Craig.

Virginia "Sue" Foreman began writing at age fifteen. Inspired by her tenth grade English teacher, she started working on her first novel, and has finally published two. Sue was born in Springfield, Ohio, where she resides. Her family moved to a farm near Mechanicsburg, Ohio at an early age, where she lived until leaving for college. After marrying her late husband and having three sons, she worked at data entry and secretarial jobs to supplement the family income when not being a full-time mom.

After raising the children and being alone for nineteen years, she met and married her current husband, adding two daughters to her family. Now in retirement, Sue has finally found time for writing, when not busy with her church, husband, and two cats.

Connie Gatlin is a retired theatre instructor and theatre director who now owns and directs a dance studio — The Cleveland City Ballet. She began her writing while serving on staff in the 1990's for what was then a start-up museum — the Museum Center at 5ive Points, which tells the story of the Ocoee Region, and the development of Cleveland and Bradley County, Tennessee. Connie is an Athena Award winner, and is currently finishing a memoir of her young days in a small Baptist church. She is the mother of Abigail, a dancer and performer, a former Rockette, and a current member of the International tour of *Beauty and the Beast*.

Janice D. Green is a wife, mother, and grandmother who retired as an elementary school library media specialist to write for children. Her writing passions include writing Bible stories, writing about God's creation, and writing family memories for the next generations. She is the owner of Honeycomb Adventures Press, LLC, and has published two Bible storybooks: *The Creation* and *The First Christmas*. She is also re-publishing Kathleen M. Muldoon's exceptional book, *Sowing Seeds: Writing for the Christian Children's Market*.

Lydia E. Harris has been married to her college sweetheart, Milt, for forty-eight years. They have two married children and five grandchildren ranging from preschool to high school. Lydia earned a Master of Arts degree in home economics. She has written numerous articles, book reviews, devotionals, and stories. Focus on the Family's *Clubhouse* magazines for children publish her recipes, which she develops and tests with her grandchildren. She writes the column, "A Cup of Tea with Lydia," and is called "Grandma Tea" by her grandchildren. Lydia has contributed to numerous books and is author of the book, *Preparing My Heart for Grandparenting: For Grandparents at Any Stage of the Journey* (AMG Publishers).

Judith Victoria Hensley is a multi-award winning retired middle school teacher, weekly newspaper columnist for the *Harlan Daily Enterprise*, freelance writer, photographer, Christian blogger (*Queen of Ordinary* and *One Step Beyond the Door*), and speaker. She has authored and edited a dozen books in Appalachian folklore, and published two middle school chapter books. Her magazine articles and short stories have appeared in a variety of publications. From her home in the Kentucky highlands, she is currently writing in a new direction of romantic Christian fiction.

Karen R. Hessen's writings have been published in six volumes of *Chicken Soup for the Soul, Guideposts, When God Makes Lemonade, RAIN Magazine 2013* and *2014, Vista* (12 times), *The Secret Place* (8 times), *The Mother's Heart Magazine, Help! I'm A Parent, God Makes Lemonade, CAP Connection, Apple Hill Cider Press, Seeds of...*, *a collection of writings by Pacific Northwest authors*" and others. She write the monthly columns, "Zap, Kackle, Plop" and "Out of the Ark" for *The Lincoln City News Guard*. The release of *Jesus Encounters* (2015) includes her latest published work. "My Best

Name" was previously published in September, 2010 in *The Mother's Heart Magazine*, which is a small ezine targeting homeschooling parents.

Julie Hilton's secret endeavor is writing. This is her first published writing and much of the story was written by her children, Russell and Jessi. She has had some drawings published and has sold many portraits, signs and murals over the years. Besides being a free-lance artist, she spent over twenty years working in the medical field. Now she is embarking on the career of a lifetime as wife and mom but continues to pursue dreams of making a difference with art and writing.

Helen Hoover enjoys sewing, reading, knitting, and traveling. She and her husband are retired, live in Northwest Arkansas, and volunteer at a Christian college. Helen's devotions and personal stories are published in books and Christian hand-out papers.

Thomas Kienzle has been married to Debra for 21 years. He has a Ph.D. in Microbiology with a specialty in Virology and is currently employed as a Virologist at a biotech company. One of his hobbies outside of work is writing fiction short stories. He is also a member of a local writing group where the focus is on creativity and critiquing members' stories. Tom has two stories in anthologies as well as one non-fiction book.

Ann Knowles, author and editor, wants the words she writes to touch hearts and make a difference in peoples' lives. She enjoys speaking and teaching at churches, retreats, and writers conferences. She delights in mentoring new writers and teaching them the craft. Visit Ann at www.writepathway.com.

Christina M. Krost is an elementary teacher turned full-time mom turned United Methodist pastor's wife. She is a congregational outreach assistant for Faith in Place, a radically inclusive Earth care non-profit. She lives with her husband and three young daughters in rural central Illinois and blogs at thekrostfamily.blogspot.com. She also leads the Mothers of Preschoolers (MOPS) group at her church, Neoga Grace United Methodist Church. When not working, chasing children, or helping minister to her church, she enjoys reading, writing, and sneaking fair trade chocolate in her closet so she doesn't have to share.

David Lehman wrote his poem, "Today It Rained Gorillas" when he was seven years old and wrote the short story, "The Accident," when he was nine years old. It depicts the true account of his accident and concussion. He is now a pastor and educator, has three children, and lives in Black Mountain North Carolina.

Yvonne Lehman is author of 55 novels. She founded, and directed for 25 years, the Blue Ridge Mountains Christian Writers Conference and now directs the Blue Ridge Novelist Retreat held annually in October at Ridgecrest NC conference center. She lives in panoramic Black Mountain North Carolina with her beautiful furry blond and white Pomeranian, Rigel, named after a Titanic survivor. Her latest books are three connected short stories in *Crashing into Love* (Lighthouse), *The Reluctant Schoolmarm* in *Reluctant Brides* collection (Barbour) and *The Stranger's Kiss* in *The Knight's Bride* collection (Barbour). Her non-fiction compilations are *Divine Moments, Christmas Moments,* and *Spoken Moments* (Grace). Her 50th book is *Hearts that Survive — A Novel of the Titanic* (Abingdon Press). She blogs with ChristiansRead and Novel Rocket.

Veronica Leigh is a Christian who lives in Indiana with her mother, sister, aunt and four fur babies. She has been published in four other anthologies and is a regular contributor to charityplaces.com's online *Femnista* magazine. She is an aspiring novelist. You can learn more about her at http://veronicaleigh.blogspot.com.

Diana Leagh Matthews is a vocalist, speaker, writer, life coach, and genealogist. She is a 2011 graduate of Christian Communicators Conference and 2012 graduate of Christian Devotions Boot Camp. She has been published in several anthologies, including *My Love to You Always, I Believe in Heaven* and *Breaking the Chains*. She currently resides in upstate South Carolina. Visit her at www.DianaLeaghMatthews.com and www.alookthrutime.com.

Beverly Hill McKinney is author of over 200 inspirational articles and two self-published books and is a graduate of the Jerry B. Jenkins Christian Writer's Guild.

Vicki H. Moss is Contributing Editor for *Southern Writers Magazine* and past Editor-at-Large. A columnist for the *American Daily Herald*, she's also a poet, author of *How to Write for Kids' Magazines* and *Writing with Voice*, a Precept Ministries Leader and a Christian Communicators graduate. She has written for *Hopscotch* and *Boy's Quest* magazines for the last decade in addition to being published in Yvonne Lehman's books *Christmas Moments* **and** *Divine Moments* (Grace), SouthWest Writer's *The Sage, Country Woman, In the City, Borderlines*, Scotland's *Thistle Blower*, and *I Believe In Heaven* by Cecil Murphey and Twila Belk. She was selected to be a presenter of her fiction and creative nonfiction short stories for three conferences in a row at the Southern Women Writers Conference held at Rome, Georgia's Berry College. Vicki is also a speaker and on faculty for writers conferences. For more information visit her at livingwaterfiction.com.

Dianna Owens is a blogger who reaches out to the community through Ignite 2 Ignite, a women's ministry. She has been published in *Living Real Magazine*. Dianna is also a full time single mom to a nine-year-old boy and four-year-old daughter. She resides in Lexington, South Carolina. Her journaling about this journey of life can be found at www.diannaowens.com.

Carole Anne Pearson is a dreamer by day and writer by night. She pursued a degree in music for two years before realizing her greater love of writing — a dream that came close on the heels of discovering her admiration for *Les Miserables*. Today, she is passionate about sharing her experiences in faith and her love of music. Carole, along with her two dogs, lives and works on her family's Mississippi cattle ranch.

Deborah M. Presnell is the author of, *Shine! Radiating the Love of God*, a nine-week study designed exclusively for young women ages 13-18. She is co-founder of Shine Ministries (Facebook: shineministriesnc) and is a partner with the Polished Conference www.polishedconference.com. She has published several articles in the *Divine Moments* series. After 30 years of teaching and more than 21 years in higher education, Debbie now spends her time writing and speaking to colleges and universities, churches, Christian women's events, as well as participating with the Polished Conference, designed for young women ages 13-18. Debbie is married and has three adult children. She resides in western North Carolina. For more information, or if you would like Debbie to speak at your next event, visit www.debbiepresnell.com.

Joey Rudder received her BFA in Creative Writing from *Bowling Green State University* and has taken ministerial courses through *Mount Vernon Nazarene University.* and Northwest Nazarene University. Her greatest classes, however, have been moments spent with the Lord: "Be still, and know that I am God" (Psalm 46:10). God has blessed her with the opportunities to write for the *Standard* (WordAction Publishing), *Country Living* magazine, to preach at her local church, and speak at ladies' functions. She has also had the privilege to write Christmas stories for over ten years to raise money for various local needs as well as the Salvation Army. Joey lives with her husband, Jim, and their ten-year-old daughter, Danika, in Sherrodsville, Ohio.

Jessica Satterfield has seen the goodness of God in the midst of the heartbreak of infertility and the joys of adoption. She is an adoption advocate and passionate about encouraging other moms throughout their journeys of motherhood. She teaches first graders, loves to write, has an eye for decorating, sews when she has time, and enjoys the beauty found in the mundane. She lives in South Carolina with her beloved, Brandon, and their two heart grown children. She helps lead the orphan care ministry at her church and adores the Lord with other women through Bible studies held in her home. Jessica's writing was published in *Adopted for Daily Life: A Devotional for Adopting Moms*. She would love for you to follow her journey at gracewhilewewait.com.

Karen Sawyer's work has appeared in *Wounded Women of the Bible*, *The Secret Place Devotional*, guest posts in *Mother Inferior* blog and *Unsent Letters* blog, *Girlfriend 2 Girlfriend* magazine, and *Montrose Anytime* magazine. She has contributed numerous articles to *ehow*, and Demand Media's other web based sites. She taught elementary school for seven years before her children were born. Karen lives in Austin, Texas, with her husband of 28 years. She is the mother of two adult children.

Kevin Spencer is a staff writer for *Christian Devotions*. A former prodigal son, Kevin now uses his gifts as an author and freelance editor, helping new writers find their way in the writing world. Kevin lives in middle Tennessee with his wife and amazing grandson, and has a life far better than he deserves.

Ann Tatlock is a two-time winner of the major Christy Award. She has also won the Midwest Independent Publishers Association "Book of the Year" in fiction for *All the Way Home* and *I'll Watch the Moon*. *Publishers Weekly* calls her "one of Christian fiction's better wordsmiths." Ann lives with her husband Asheville, North Carolina.

C. Kevin Thompson is a member of the Christian Authors Network (CAN), American Christian Fictions Writers (ACFW), and Word Weavers International. He is the Chapter President of Word Weavers-Lake County (Florida). His published works include two award-winning novels: *The Serpent's Grasp* (Winner of the 2013 Blue Ridge Mountain Christian Writers Conference Selah Award for First Fiction), and *30 Days Hath Revenge - A Blake Meyer Thriller: Book 1*. His articles appear in *The Wesleyan Advocate*, *The Preacher*, *Vista*, *The Des Moines Register* and *The Ocala Star-Banner*. Kevin is a huge fan of the TV series *24*, *The Blacklist*, *Blue Bloods*, and *Criminal Minds*, loves anything to do with *Star Trek*, and is a Sherlock Holmes fanatic, too. You can visit Kevin @ www.ckevinthompson.com.

Carol Weeks is a Christian humorist, Certified Laughter Leader, speaker and author. Her blog, *Carol Weeks Speaks!*, is updated every Friday. She has contributed stories used by best-selling author Liz Curtis Higgs in two books, been highlighted in Vicki H. Moss' column for The *American Daily Herald*, and has a devotion in 2014's *Penned from the Heart*. She's a member of the Fellowship of Christian Bloggers, a 2012 graduate of Christian Communicators Conference and a 2013 graduate of Christian Communicators Conference Advanced.

Cindy Wilson received her Nursing degree from Western Carolina University and is a Clinical Auditor for a local hospital. She and her husband of twenty-seven years live in South Carolina with their teenage son. The articles, "Peace" and "Growth" in *Spoken Moments,* are her first publications.

Steve Wilson wrote the poem, "First Things" after the miscarriage of his and Cindy's child. The poem was included in "Christmas Tradition," one of three short stories in *Crashing into Christmas* (LPC). Steve is a graphic designer holding the position of Advertising Director at the company where he works.

Jean Wilund is a writer, teacher and blogger. She's passionate about travel, sports, and coffee, but mostly about sharing the life-giving truths in God's Word. She's been published in Focus on the Family's *Clubhouse, Jr.* magazine and in *Reach Out, Columbia* magazine. She blogs weekly about the journey of faith in Christ on *Join the Journey* at www.JeanWilund.com. She's the founding president of the Lexington, SC Chapter of Word Weavers International and a member of Palmetto Christian Writer's Network, Society of Children's Book Writers and Illustrators and My Book Therapy. Jean and Larry, her husband of over 30 years, live in Lexington, South Carolina have three grown children.

Felicity Younts was born on a starry night in Colorado in the spring of 2007. Since her birth she's had many military brat adventures until her hero daddy decided to settle his family in the sweetest place on earth in the heart of Pennsylvania. Felicity is the daughter of author Elizabeth Byler Younts. Though before writing "The Legend of the Weeping Willow" she insisted she was not a writer, she now has plans to write many more stories. Felicity's most prized possession is her cat Babushka. Her favorite authors are E.B. White and C.S. Lewis. When not working on her homeschool lessons Felicity can be found adventuring with her sister Mercy to find magic worlds in wardrobes.

www.ingramcontent.com/pod-product-compliance
Lightning Source LLC
Chambersburg PA
CBHW060533100426
42743CB00009B/1518